Selected Writings of
PIERRE-JOSEPH PROUDHON

STEWART EDWARDS, born in 1937, read History at Selwyn College, Cambridge University, and did his postgraduate research at the London School of Economics and in Paris. He is a Lecturer in Political Theory at the University of Southampton, and has been a visiting Assistant Professor at the State University of New York at Buffalo.

ELIZABETH FRASER is a Lecturer in French Literature, University of Southampton. She received her undergraduate and graduate degrees at the University of Wales.

Selected *Writings* of
PIERRE-JOSEPH PROUDHON

EDITED WITH
AN INTRODUCTION BY
STEWART EDWARDS
TRANSLATED BY
ELIZABETH FRASER

"Old Proudhon's visions of darkness and evil . . ."
— Saul Bellow, *Herzog*

MACMILLAN

First published in the United States of America 1969
First published in the United Kingdom 1970

Published by
MACMILLAN AND CO LTD
Little Essex Street London WC2
and also at Bombay Calcutta and Madras
Macmillan South Africa (Publishers) Pty Ltd Johannesburg
The Macmillan Company of Australia Pty Ltd Melbourne
The Macmillan Company of Canada Ltd Toronto
Gill and Macmillan Ltd Dublin

Printed in Great Britain by
LOWE AND BRYDONE (PRINTERS) LTD
London

Contents

6   *Contents*

PREFACE

Proudhon's name is found in most studies and anthologies of anarchism and of nineteenth-century socialist thought. But the reader of English has little chance to examine Proudhon's writings themselves, as translations have been made of only three of his earliest books.[1] The present selection attempts to provide a survey of the main themes found in Proudhon's writings across a period of twenty-five years, with an emphasis on his political and social ideas. Such an emphasis reflects Proudhon's own view of himself as an anarchist and socialist, or "mutualist," and this is the cause of his greatest renown.

Proudhon's discursive style makes cutting both easy and, often, necessary, since for an outline of his views his arguments can be lifted clear of the digressions and examples which make up much of the body of his work. For a fuller example of his style see one of the complete translations listed in the Bibliography.

Mr. William Pickles of the London School of Economics first introduced me to the writings of Proudhon, and has been most generous with advice and criticism during the preparation of this selection, both in the editing and

[1] A selection of his writings on free credit was published in 1927, and the 1888 translation of *What Is Property* has recently been reprinted. See Bibliography.

in the translation. Professor James Joll also kindly read the Introduction, and I am very grateful for his comments and encouragement. Mr. I. K. Fraser most freely gave of his expert knowledge in helping to translate Proudhon's legal terms. Mr. E. E. Papst and Mr. M. E. Pountney kindly responded to appeals for help in preparing a manuscript from both sides of the Atlantic. The staff of the Salle des Catalogues of the Bibliothèque nationale and of the University of Buffalo's Lockwood Memorial Library were always ready to assist in tracing the many references found in Proudhon's allusive style. Acknowledgments are due to the Foreign Languages Publishing House, Moscow, for permission to use their translation (with a few changes) of Marx's letter to Proudhon from *Karl Marx and Frederick Engels: Selected Correspondence*, Moscow, 1956, pp. 32–33; and to Marcel Rivière for permission to use their edition of Proudhon's *Carnets*, ed. P. Haubtmann, Paris, 1960, vol. 2, p. 337.

NOTE ON THE TEXT
AND ABBREVIATIONS

The new edition of the *Oeuvres complètes de P.-J. Proudhon*, published by Marcel Rivière under the general editorship of C. Bouglé and H. Moysset (Paris, 1920 to date), has been used as the French text wherever possible. In this collection the volume of *Du Principe fédératif* includes also *La Fédération et l'unité en Italie;* and the volume entitled *Contradictions politiques* includes in addition to the *Théorie de mouvement constitutionnel au XIXe siècle, Les Démocrates assermentés et les réfractaires* and *Si les Traités de 1815 ont cessé d'exister?*

The following editions have been used for works of Proudhon not included at present in the Bouglé-Moysset collection:

Correspondance, 14 vols., Paris, 1875.
Du Principe de l'art et de sa destination sociale, oeuvres posthumes, Paris, 1865.
Manuel du spéculateur à la Bourse, vol. 11 of the *Oeuvres complètes,* Paris, 1869.
Solution du problème social, vol. 6 of the *Oeuvres complètes,* Paris, 1868.
Théorie de l'impôt, vol. 15 of the *Oeuvres complètes,* Paris, 1868.
Théorie de la propriété, 2nd ed., Paris, 1866.

All volume and page references in the text are to one of the above editions.

The following abbreviations have been used in the references, the dates in parentheses included in the text being the dates of first publication, or, in the case of the post-humous *Theory of Property* and *Political Contradictions,* the approximate date of composition.

Art (1865)	*On the Principle of Art (Du Principe de l'art et de sa destination sociale)*
C	*Correspondence,* 14 vols.
Confessions (1849)	*Confessions of a Revolutionary (Les Confessions d'un révolutionnaire)*
Creation (1843)	*The Creation of Order in Humanity (De la Création de l'order dans l'humanité)*
Democrats (1863)	*Oath-taking Democrats and Non-Jurors (Les Démocrates assermentés et les réfractaires)*
Econ. Contrads. (1846)	*System of Economic Contradictions or the Philosophy of Poverty (Système des Contradictions économiques ou Philosophie de la misère),* 2 vols.
Fed. (1863)	*The Federal Principle (Du Principe fédératif)*
Italy (1862)	*Federation and Unity in Italy (La Fédération et l'unité en Italie)*
Justice (1858)	*Justice in the Revolution and the Church (De la Justice dans la Révolution et dans l'Église),* 4 vols.
Manual (1857)	*Manual for the Stock-Exchange Speculator (Manuel du spéculateur à la Bourse)*
Memoir (1840)	*What Is Property? First Memoir (Qu'est-ce que la Propriété? Premier mémoire)*
Pol. Cap. (1865)	*On the Political Capacity of the Working Classes (De la capacité politique des classes ouvrières)*

Pol. Contrads. (1863–64)	*Political Contradictions: Theory of the Constitutional Movement in the 19th Century (Contradictions politiques: Théorie du mouvement constitutionnel au XIX*e *siècle)*
Progress (1853)	*Philosophy of Progress (Philosophie du Progrès)*
Property (1863–64)	*Theory of Property (Théorie de la propriété)*
Revn. (1851)	*General Idea of Revolution in the 19th Century (Idée générale de la Révolu- au XIX*e *siècle)*
Solution (1848–49)	*Solution of the Social Problem (Solution du problème social)*
Taxation (1861)	*Theory of Taxation (Théorie de l'impôt)*
Treaties (1863)	*What if the Treaties of 1815 Ceased to Exist? (Si les Traités de 1815 ont cessé d'exister?)*
War (1861)	*War and Peace (La Guerre et la paix)*

Proudhon's own capitals, italics, parentheses, and occasional use of three suspension points (...) have been kept, as has Proudhon's practice of following the custom of referring to the Revolutionary years of 1789, 1793, 1796, 1830, and 1848 as '89, '93, etc. Editorial ellipsis is indicated by four dots (. . . .) to mark a break in the text. Passages in square brackets [] have been inserted by the editor.

Introduction

Pierre-Joseph Proudhon (1809–65) is usually regarded as one of the first anarchist writers, and as an early socialist theorist. In his early works, especially previous to the establishment of Napoleon III's Second Empire, he radically attacked the existing economic and political system. On the other hand, Proudhon's social ideas after the 1850s were sufficiently reactionary for a French right-wing nationalist, Louis Dimier, to be able to include Proudhon as one of the "masters of the counter-revolution in the nineteenth century."[1] Proudhon did not leave behind an established body of followers. Rather, his ideas were taken up separately by different sections of the French political spectrum from the syndicalists on the Left to the nationalists on the Right. In his first letter after the February Revolution of 1848, Proudhon expressed his sense of isolation from his contemporaries.[2] He remained an isolated figure during the Second Empire, though his name was often invoked by Vermorel, Tolain, and other French working-class leaders. He also knew some of the literary notables of his time, including Sainte-Beuve, who published the first appreciation of Proudhon.[3]

[1] L. Dimier, *Les Maîtres de la contre-révolution au* XIXe *siècle,* Paris, 1907.

[2] Letter of February 25, 1848: see below, p. 155.

[3] P.-J. Proudhon, *Sa Vie et sa Correspondance,* Paris, 1866.

Life

More than is the case with many theorists, Proudhon's writings are dominated by his personality. He was
born in Besançon, both his parents being of Franc-Comtois
peasant stock. His father was at first a tavern keeper who
brewed his own beer, and Proudhon worked for a time as
his father's cellar-boy.[4] But business failed and the family
moved in Proudhon's eighth year to the farm of his
mother's family a few miles from Besançon, where the
young boy roamed the fields and mountains as a cowherd
in the French Jura. After a few years' schooling, his
family's poverty forced him to find work and he became
an apprentice in 1827 at the Besançon press, owned by
the family of his schoolfriend, Antoine Gauthier, and
which being the diocesan press gave Proudhon occasion
to read theology. But like most first-generation industrial
workers, Proudhon kept as his ideal the peasant life he
had known as a boy, and there is in Proudhon a sense of
the marriage of the laborer to the soil, a mystique of the
land, similar to that found in Michelet or Tolstoy (both
of whom Proudhon knew).

For the next few years Proudhon was in effect a *com-
pagnon* of the *"tour de France,"* one of the many journeymen wandering from town to town taking whatever employment could be obtained. He spent some time in both
Paris and Lyon before returning to Besançon, where he
entered into partnership in a small printing firm. As with
Rousseau, it was a university prize competition, in this
case for the University of Besançon on *Sunday Observance*
(1839), that gave Proudhon his first real opportunity to
express some of his ideas. Proudhon followed this up with
his *First Memoir* on property, *What Is Property?* (1840).

[4] Cf. below, p. 48.

This begins with the arresting statement that property is theft,[5] as dramatic an opening as that of Rousseau's *Social Contract*. The *First Memoir* quickly made Proudhon's reputation and he only just escaped prosecution, but, as with an earlier anarchist work, Godwin's *Political Justice* (1793), it was considered that the book would appeal only to "high intelligences and cultivated minds." However, Proudhon's next book, *A Warning to Property Owners* (1842), was seized, though the jury acquitted him because they found his ideas too difficult to follow.

In 1843 he sold his press at Besançon and returned to his schoolfriend Gauthier's firm, this time as a secretary in Lyon. It was at this time that he came into contact with the co-operative ideas of the Lyon silk workers. During a visit to Paris in the winter of 1844–45 Proudhon was introduced to the ideas of the German Left-Hegelians and met many of the foreign exiles there, including Bakunin and Marx.

Proudhon moved permanently to Paris just before the overthrow of the monarchy of Louis Philippe in February 1848. By this time Proudhon was recognized as a leading radical and socialist thinker (as the words were used then), though one who had made his name more as a critic than as an ally of the other socialists and democrats of the time, such as Louis Blanc, Pierre Leroux, Victor Considérant (the leader of the Fourierists), Étienne Cabet, and Lamennais. Although Proudhon did not in general approve of the February Revolution he was soon caught up by events. He was a speaker at many of the popular clubs that had been formed. He published several pamphlets expounding his ideas on the organization of credit, which he tried to put into practice by founding a People's Bank.[6] And he reached a wide audience among the Paris democrats through his paper *Le Repré-*

[5] Cf. below, p. 124.
[6] Cf. below, pp. 75–80.

sentant du Peuple, later called *La Voix du Peuple.* He was even elected to the National Assembly in June 1848. The rising by unemployed Paris workers in this same month struck terror into the hearts of bourgeois republicans, who until then had been only too willing to use the Paris crowds in overthrowing French monarchies. Proudhon soon came to be regarded by the Government and his fellow deputies as a dangerous revolutionary, inciting the French workers to revolt by his attacks on property, religion and the family. An article criticizing the newly elected President of the year-old Republic, Louis Napoleon, led to Proudhon's condemnation. While in hiding he managed to fulfill his betrothal of two years previously, and he was married just before the police arrested him.

Proudhon was still in prison when Louis Napoleon's *coup d'état* of December 1851 led to the establishment of the Second Empire. As a result, police control and censorship became much stricter. Hence when Proudhon was freed in 1852 he was unable to get published the ideas which now more than ever he wanted to express. Politically, there was no longer the exciting sense of almost limitless possibilities, which had marked French social thinkers during the previous regime, and Proudhon's tragic vision became more prominent in the books he wrote in the period after the late 1850s. Privately, he had difficulties in trying to support his wife and daughters by writing an occasional article or pamphlet (unsigned of course) or by dabbling in some business affairs with a few of his old friends.

In 1858 Proudhon managed to persuade Garniers to publish his first full-length book since his imprisonment, *De la Justice,* which he had begun as a reply to an attack on him by a Catholic pamphleteer. Financially this was an immediate success, but before the last few copies of the first edition were sold out they were seized by the police and Proudhon was charged with "attacking the rights of the family, outraging public and religious morality and disrespecting the law." In order to avoid a possible further term in prison, Proudhon went into exile in Brussels. Here he stayed even after Napoleon III's political amnesty, remaining until 1862 when he was forced to leave by the local population, enraged because of certain remarks he made about Belgium in an article on nationalism.[7] During this time abroad Proudhon wrote *War and Peace, Theory of Taxation,* and an enlarged second edition of *Justice.* Back in Paris, he expanded his pamphlet on nationalism into *Federation and Unity in Italy,* and then he developed this argument further in *The Federal Principle* (1863). The "Manifesto of the Sixty" Paris workers[8] turned Proudhon's attention back to industrial affairs in France, especially as several working-class groups had written to him asking for his reaction to the Manifesto. He dictated the last pages of his reply from his deathbed, and the book, *On the Political Capacity of the Working Classes,* came out shortly after his death in 1865. A crowd of several thousand accompanied him to his grave in the cemetery of Passy.

Thought and Influence

Proudhon was not a trained philosopher, but an autodidact whose knowledge came from his wide if unselective reading. He wrote only one systematic work of metaphysics, *The Creation of Order in Humanity* (1843), and in his other works philosophical theories are mixed with social analyses. Like many other nineteenth-century writers, Proudhon believed that philosophy, politics and morality needed an entirely new basis, which he sought to provide. Accepting his fellow townsman Fourier's

[7] See below, p. 191.
[8] Cf. below, p. 171.

notion of a "serial law of development" throughout the universe, which Proudhon termed "serial dialectic"[9], Proudhon began his social philosophy with the assumption that laws of development applied both to the material world and to human society, and that the discovery of these laws would turn economics and politics into a science. In seeking for the laws which govern society Proudhon was thus in the tradition (as he himself realized) of Montesquieu and Saint-Simon, who have often been regarded among the founders of sociology.[10]

Marx claimed to have "infected" Proudhon with Hegelianism during their acquaintanceship in Paris at the end of 1844. At this time Proudhon was a well-known socialist writer while Marx, nine years younger, was an unknown revolutionary exile from Germany, and it is hardly surprising that Proudhon did not retain much of Marx's interpretation of Hegel. On the other hand, Marx had been greatly impressed by Proudhon's earlier work, *What Is Property?*, and he considered that Proudhon was one of the first "scientific socialist" writers. It was presumably with this opinion that Marx, after he had left Paris, proposed to Proudhon that they should continue to exchange ideas. But Proudhon rejected this suggestion, suspecting that Marx would not tolerate views different from his own, especially as Proudhon had already developed his own particular interpretation of Hegel.[11]

Another German visitor to Proudhon in Paris had been Karl Grün, who had been converted by Moses Hess to the atheist humanism of Feuerbach. Proudhon's early theo-

[9] Cf. below, p. 226.

[10] On Proudhon as a sociologist see C. Bouglé, *La sociologie de Proudhon*, Paris, 1911; G. Gurvitch, *Proudhon, sa vie, son oeuvre*, Collection Philosophes, Paris, 1965, pp. 31–46; P. Ansart, *Sociologie de Proudhon*, Paris, 1967. In Proudhon, as in Marx or Durkheim, social analysis is linked to proposals for social reform.

[11] Marx and Proudhon's letters of 1846: see below, pp. 147–54.

logical interests made him suggestive to the Feuerbachian notion that religion was the alienation of man's inherent human values. By January 1845 Proudhon was writing that he had been persuaded by a "large number of Germans" of the importance of Hegel, and that in his next book he would seek to apply Hegel's dialectic to economics.[12] This appeared in 1846 as *The System of Economic Contradictions or the Philosophy of Poverty*, which Marx at once attacked by publishing in French his *Poverty of Philosophy*.

Proudhon used the Kantian term "antinomy" as equivalent in meaning to "contradiction." Truth is never wholly one thing to the exclusion of its opposite; it is the movement between seeming opposites. True to his interest in the Greeks, Proudhon often began by seeking the *telos* or "aim" of the subject under inquiry, which he sometimes looked for in the terminology of the French legal code.[13] Proudhon then sought to show how this original purpose could no longer be attained within the existing social order, and that there was a contradiction between the end and existing practice. For example, in *War and Peace* (Tolstoy borrowed more than just the title from Proudhon's work)[14] war is described as an expression of the

[12] Letter to Bergmann, January 19, 1845: *Correspondance*, vol. 2, pp. 175–76.

[13] See for example pp. 105–6, 131, 137 below.

[14] Tolstoy had read Proudhon's *First Memoir* on property of 1840, and had been struck by Proudhon's anarchist ideas and by his attack on the notion of property. In 1861 Tolstoy obtained a letter of introduction from Alexander Herzen and visited Proudhon in Brussels just as Proudhon was completing *La Guerre et la paix*. Tolstoy seems to have been influenced by certain of the ideas in this book in forming his own philosophy of history as set out in the novel, which when completed he called *War and Peace* after Proudhon's work: see further Henri Troyat, *Tolstoy*, New York, 1967, pp. 205, 274, 297; E. J. Simmons, *Leo Tolstoy*, Vintage Books, New York, 1960, vol. 1, pp. 180, 213–14.

strife that lies at the root of society. But then Proudhon goes on to argue that war is no longer historically justified and that it should be replaced by economic competition within the balance of power established by the treaties of 1815. In the *System of Economic Contradictions* Proudhon describes Capitalism (and its interpreters, the classical free-trade economists) and Socialism as two such antinomies. The conflict between them must be resolved into a new synthesis, Mutualism, which would "resolve" the antinomy between the socialists' ideas of Justice and the economists' "laws" of production and exchange.

This search for an equilibrium in all things can easily be lost among the many passages of polemic that are so striking in Proudhon's writings. He is easily carried away by words and by the fascination of arguing a case, even if he later rejects it. Sometimes he plays the Devil's advocate so well that his real views are obscured. In writing *War and Peace*, for example, Proudhon moves from a justifiable emphasis on the importance of struggle and conflict in the development of society and civilization to a glorification of war comparable to the ennoblement of violence found in later fascist movements.

Proudhon always sought to reveal the clash of opposing forces, and this eventually led him away from the Hegelian idea of a dialectical progress through history in which opposites are resolved into a new synthesis. Instead, Proudhon came to argue that opposites must balance each other; the antinomies are not resolved as he had thought earlier.[15] Property, for example, balances the power of the State; authority and liberty must likewise balance each other. For this reason Miguel de Unamuno has

[15] Cf. below, pp. 227–29: though in the *Creation of Order* (written before his meeting with the German Hegelians in Paris) Proudhon talks of his "ideo-realist" metaphysics; namely, that there are a number of different "series" of laws in the universe, and that these cannot be resolved into some higher order of ideas: cf. below, pp. 226–27.

compared Proudhon to Pascal (whom Proudhon often quoted), saying that Pascal's "logic was by no means a form of dialectic, but rather a polemic; he did not seek a synthesis betwixt thesis and antithesis; he persisted, as did Proudhon (another Pascalian in his way) in contradiction."[16] In effect Proudhon argued that there are certain inherent social instincts in men, such as the desire to own property, whereas Marx argued, in attacking Proudhon, that such desires were solely the effect of a certain order of economic relations and would be changed if men lived under a different social system.

Proudhon considered that the task of the philosopher, or of the social scientist, was to set out the structure of ideas, or forms, of any given society: to show, for example, that a hierarchical religion, Catholicism, was the counterpart of a hierarchical system of secular government, and that this in turn corresponded to the hierarchical organization found within a factory. Society was held together by such laws, or "ideas," though these could not be reduced to one general law. Any change within one sphere would be reflected by similar changes in the other spheres.

Such a series of changes made up the movement of progress in history, a movement which Proudhon often called "the Revolution" (always in the singular). Prouhon's idea here is that societies have a nature, or, as Aristotle put it, that they are in *phusis*. Whatever happens is to be seen as an unfolding of what is in that nature. This is a fundamental tenet of classical evolutionism. Applied to society, it is the view that an analysis of what is potential or latent in society will yield a description of future social development. But instead of the will of God or the Spirit of History it is the collective will of mankind which Proudhon saw as the final absolute. Justice can only come through the man-made laws of a just

[16] *The Agony of Christianity,* Eng. trans., New York, 1928, p. 134.

society, and social science is the theory of the progressive
development of Justice,[17] or of the Revolution. Proudhon's idea of the Revolution could well be taken as another example of the rationalist approach to politics.[18]
What previously had been only a half-conscious tradition
becomes a conscious design: politics is replaced by social
science.[19]

Proudhon limited himself to seeking an analysis of the
processes at work in French society, for he believed (as
many French writers have) that the future of Europe
could be read in the history of France. The French Revolution was seen, therefore, as the turning point in European history. Before 1789, societies changed by a process
of Immanence. But with the French Revolution this immanent development of history becomes conscious. Society
no longer develops "organically"; instead, men now delib-
erately seek to organize society according to the principles
of Justice. It is the conscience of mankind that dictates
to reason the principles of Justice by which men understand and judge the world, a view which Proudhon opposed to that of the Church, which had set God over the
world in order to reveal the law to man. The Revolution of
1789 had tried to mold society according to the principles
of liberty and equality. France had become a democracy
politically but not economically, and the French Revolution had failed because it limited itself to political reforms.
The task of the Revolution in the nineteenth century was
to extend these two principles from the political to the
economic order. This is what Proudhon meant when he
said that politics must give way to economics.[20]

17 Proudhon's use of the term Justice is comparable to that of
Aristotle; in both, Justice is the good aimed at in the State: cf.
The Politics, Bk. I, 1253a, and Bk. III, 1282b.
18 See Michael Oakeshott, *Rationalism in Politics and Other
Essays,* London, 1962.
19 Cf. below, pp. 237–39, 243.
20 Cf. below, pp. 90–91.

In his *First Memoir on Property* (1840) Proudhon defined capitalist exploitation in terms of a "miscalculation"
(*erreur de compte*). Like Marx, Proudhon accepted the
labor theory of value of the British classical economists.
The capitalist pays alike the day's labor of one hundred
workers or the labor of one worker for one hundred days.
Yet, argued Proudhon, the value produced is not the same
in each case, and to count the work done by an individual
as the same as that done by a group ignores the "collective
force" of the latter.[21] Factory production is a social method
of production, and society should be organized accordingly
as a system of exchange between associations of producers.
Rather than following the ideas of association or co-
operative production, which were popular in the 1840s,
Proudhon's "mutualism" is a socialism of credit and exchange. This new idea of "mutuality" would become the
dominant pattern of all future social relationships. But
under the present system there is a conflict (or a "contradiction") between the social system of production and the
individualistic system of buying and selling. This conflict,
the result of an unjust economic system, had to be contained by a strong central power, and so an oppressive
economic system engendered an oppressive State. Political
despotism was both a result and a support of the capitalists' exploitation of the collective labor of the workers. This
led Proudhon to argue for the abolition of the State as a
necessary accompaniment to any reform of the economic
order.

Proudhon followed Rousseau in arguing that the State
originated in a deception of the majority by a self-
interested minority. Mankind had come to believe that
the State had a strength of its own, as seen in its armies
and public officials. But all its apparent power came from
the alienation of the "collective force." Once men had
recovered the power they alone had created, then the

[21] Cf. below, pp. 42–46.

State would be seen as it really was, simply a façade. Justice could come only when men received the full value of their labor, instead of having to be a party to their own exploitation.[22] This rejection of the State, which Proudhon called anarchism, separated him from most other critics of capitalism, who favored using the State's power to organize the workers into associations, to run public works, or to crush the capitalists.

With relationships of authority removed from the system of production and thus from politics, all relationships would be simply contractual. Proudhon defined such a contract as synallagmatic and commutative: that is to say, a contract in which each party is equally obliged to the other and one in which the exchange is between goods of equal value. This is the basis of "mutualism," which is, said Proudhon, the old principle of an eye for an eye and a tooth for a tooth applied to economic and political relationships.[23]

Proudhon was at pains to distinguish his notion of contract from that of Rousseau or Hobbes. Both, according to Proudhon, treated the contract as one made between individuals or between individuals and the Sovereign, and this led to the subjugation of the individual to the State. Proudhon would have agreed that the only result of the Hobbesian state of nature could be a society ruled by an absolute sovereign, for Proudhon firmly believed that, left to himself, the individual tries to gain absolute power over others. The lack of justice in political and economic relations comes from this self-seeking. But where there is no economic repression there is no need for a sovereign power in society to ensure that men keep their contracts.[24] Instead, freed of authoritarian economic relationships men would no longer seek purely selfish ends and the "collec-

[22] Cf. below, pp. 113–22.
[23] Cf. below, p. 60.
[24] Cf. below, pp. 57–61.

tive reason" would produce Justice in society. Proudhon's idea of a "collective force" distinct from the egoism of individuals is closer to a sociological understanding of society than is the atomistic approach of Hobbes. It invites comparison with Rousseau's distinction between the "General Will" and the "Will of All," and it is clear that Proudhon was not so different from Rousseau as he claimed to be.

Proudhon rejected any comparison between the body politic and the human organism. Such comparisons lead to the notion of a hierarchy in the State (as in Saint Paul's use of this metaphor), whereas Proudhon insisted, like Rousseau, that men are by nature equal.[25] Much of the supposed inequality between men is simply the result of social custom, which has been formed by the parasites of society who consider themselves superior to those who labor, or by bureaucrats and administrators who award honors to themselves. Inequality is also the result of differences in education. Proudhon attacked the overspecialization forced on workers by factory conditions. Instead, the young worker should be apprenticed to many trades to avoid becoming merely a human tool incapable of more than one task. All education, Proudhon thought, should be a mixture of study of the arts and sciences along with work in the fields and factories.[26]

[25] Cf. below, pp. 52, 66–67.

[26] Cf. below, pp. 80–88. This notion of a "practical education" is found in other writings of this time, and expresses a desire to escape from the specialization of the division of labor and the formation of an educated and an uneducated class that follows. The editor of one of the first working-class newspapers in Paris in the 1840s, Anthyme Corbon (of the *Atelier*), published a book on *Professional Education* in 1859. The same idea is found in the reports of the workers' delegations to the Great Exhibitions of 1862 (in London) and 1867 (in Paris). The French delegates to the Congresses of the First International at Geneva in 1866 and Brussels in 1868 put forward explicitly Proudhonian ideas on education: see further G. Du-

Proudhon did not argue in favor of complete equality, however, and he attacked the French socialist writers of the 1840s on the grounds that their doctrines were too egalitarian. Proudhon's ideal was rather the mean. The industrious should be awarded proportionately more than the lazy, but differences in rewards should never become great enough to produce the wide extremes of wealth and power which Proudhon attacked in the name of equality. Social harmony would come when all approached one common level. For Proudhon held that if men limited their needs to those of the simple life of the land, then nature had provided sufficient for all.

Commerce and trade, therefore, were attacked by Proudhon as cosmopolitan evils, which threatened the natural patriotism that should hold a country together. To belong to a nation or community meant sharing the sacrifices imposed on it by the need to support its own population. A government was obliged to protect its national industry and agriculture, just as it had the duty of guarding the national territory. Free trade, on the other hand, Proudhon argued, could only lead to greater unemployment among the French working class, a fear that has often been expressed during the history of the labor movement. It was, therefore, in the name of Louis Blanc's socialist slogan of the "right to work" that Proudhon was able to defend his protectionist views.[27]

Through all his writings there runs the same strong moralism that was characteristic of his personal life.[28]

veau, *La Pensée ouvrière sur l'éducation,* Paris, 1947, pp. 103–22, 320 (and for Proudhon's own views on education, pp. 147–59).

[27] Cf. below, p. 187.

[28] Sainte-Beuve, op. cit., Preface and Ch. 4, speaks of Proudhon's "moral uprightness," and says Proudhon always preserved his "moral integrity and strength of intelligence"; cf. further Proudhon's writings on the purpose of art and on the family: pp. 214–17, 254–56 below.

He condemned luxury; idleness was a vice, work a virtue. Like many other socialists and anarchists, Proudhon believed that labor in itself was a good. Where he differed from theorists such as Fourier, Marx, or Kropotkin, was in his gloom regarding the necessity of toil. Industrialization, he held, would never change the lot of man, which was to labor in poverty, and Proudhon scorned any doctrine of the automatic improvement of mankind. Capitalist society was as cruel in its way as medieval feudalism or classical antiquity had been. The Christian doctrine of original sin was interpreted by Proudhon as a symbol of man's ineradicable tendency toward evil, rejecting Rousseau's doctrine of the natural goodness of men. All that could be done, Proudhon held, was to seek to create a social order in which men's evil inclinations would be held in check. His praise of work came partly from his conviction that idleness and leisure could only provide occasions for vice. Man, like the rest of the universe, was a victim of opposing forces and society had to accommodate this opposition, not seek to avoid it. Here again, Proudhon showed himself closer to conservatives such as de Maistre than to socialist or liberal writers.

This conservatism became increasingly apparent in Proudhon's later writings. As a result of the Crimean War, Proudhon became much more interested in foreign affairs. At the same time he grew increasingly depressed as he observed the internal consolidation of the Napoleonic Government's power. France seemed to be returning to the centralized absolutism of the *ancien régime*—a view also shared by de Tocqueville. Proudhon coined the term "Industrial Empire" to describe this regime in which an army of administrators maintained order and exploited the nation in the interests of a few financiers and industrialists.[29] Heading this new feudal hierarchy was the Em-

[29] Cf. below, p. 166. Marx too remarked on this same phenomenon in his *Eighteenth Brumaire*.

peror, conducting what Proudhon regarded as a largely disastrous foreign policy.

The later Proudhon believed that the nation State was such a threat to individual liberty that only constitutional safeguards could protect the citizen from losing all his rights. He still argued that society consisted of relations between independent economic groups, but now he saw society as an equilibrium between central and local powers. He was sure that no society could exist without some element of authority, which could only be balanced, never entirely removed. To resist the tendency of all power to accumulate more power, society must be broken up into a number of autonomous units.

"Mutualist" associations of producers would be linked into communes, which would make up a federation. Not all production should be organized in the form of associations. In his final theory of property Proudhon exempted agricultural production, where the group would be the family, and he did not see any reason to organize trade collectively. Nor were trade-union associations acceptable, as these were a counterweight to the power of neither the State nor big business. Very much the opposite, for Proudhon considered that the trade-union movement presented a new danger. It would lead to a society divided between organized capital and organized labor, and in this process the medium-sized producer—merchant or peasant—would be crushed.[30] No unit, neither the State nor the factory, should be big enough to engender an oppressive and hierarchical organization. And throughout all his writings Proudhon opposed the democrats; he considered that no representative system of government could protect the interests of the individual. It was size that Proudhon saw as the main danger to men's liberty.

These same federal or mutualist principles provided the theoretical justification for Proudhon's opposition to the

[30] Cf. below, pp. 180–83.

national movements in Poland, Hungary, and Italy. Proudhon could hardly have been sympathetic to nationalist leaders such as Mazzini, who wanted to form Italy into a strongly centralized power. Nor could Proudhon favor movements that he considered were led by the national aristocracy and financiers, who were against the interests of the peasantry in whom Proudhon saw the only hope for a revolution in his sense. Applied to Poland, this reasoning distinguished Proudhon from Marx and from most European revolutionaries and liberals, who considered an independent Poland a progressive step toward reducing the reactionary power of the Tsar in Europe.

But Proudhon also judged foreign affairs, as he admitted himself, from the viewpoint of France's national interest. This was particularly explicit with regard to Italy. Proudhon realized that the expulsion of Austria from Italy would not necessarily cause the influence of France there to increase. The growth of a strong, united Italy would end France's role as the major Catholic power in Europe. And so Proudhon, who had been exiled in 1858 for attacking Catholicism in his *Justice in the Revolution and the Church,* defended Napoleon III's support of the Pope against Garibaldi and the King of Sardinia.[31]

As Jaurès said, Proudhon was so completely French that he wished to prevent the formation of new nations on France's frontiers.[32] Proudhon was interested in European affairs only insofar as they affected France. Whereas Marx, for example, had no hesitation in discussing affairs outside Germany, Proudhon was glad to return to France in 1861, after his exile in Belgium, because he could again observe the social and political developments of his time from the viewpoint of his own country. For, as he said, he

[31] Cf. below, pp. 188–90.
[32] *L'Armée nouvelle,* new ed., Paris, 1932, p. 374. Jean Jaurès was the first leader of the French Socialist Party (S.F.I.O.) from its formation in 1905 to his assassination on the eve of the First World War.

B*

could only comment on affairs with a "French accent."[33]
For the same reason, Proudhon had earlier refused offers
of help in escaping from France after Napoleon III's *coup
d'état*.[34] Instead, just after his release from prison in 1852,
Proudhon, in *The Social Revolution as exemplified by the
coup d'état of December 2nd*, sought to defend his "unhappy country" against its foreign detractors, especially
the "Jacobin Mazzini," who had dared to suggest that
France had forfeited her role as the leader of the revolution in Europe.[35] Although Proudhon later became a
bitter critic of the Imperial regime, he never considered
that any other nation could replace France as the expression of the Revolutionary Idea. This messianic belief
in the destiny of his country was one of the few traces
Proudhon carried over from his association with the democrats of the 1840s. If France was doomed, as Proudhon
in despair sometimes believed, then the rest of Europe
was even more so. And if France could not regenerate
herself, then the French socialists should, in the words
of Racine's Hermione, choose to die with their own country rather than to live in any other.[36]

It is hardly surprising that French nationalist writers of
the turn of this century picked up Proudhon as the only
purely French socialist and used his name to attack the
Marxist doctrines of international socialism. They interpreted the history of the Second International as an attempt by the Marxist German Social Democrats to exploit
French socialism in the interests of the German Empire,
while commending Proudhon as an example of "French
socialism" and of "the French national tradition."[37]

[33] Letter of April 25, 1861: *Correspondance,* Vol. 11, p. 35.
[34] See further R. Labry, *Herzen et Proudhon,* Paris, 1928,
pp. 126–33.
[35] Letter of March 1852: *Correspondance,* Vol. 4, pp. 263–
64; *Du Principe Fédératif,* p. 517.
[36] *De la Justice,* Vol. 4., p. 426.
[37] Jean Darville in *Cahiers du Cercle Proudhon,* Paris, 1912–
13, p. 10. See too the extended development of this argument

As has been seen, Proudhon never became actively involved in politics except for short periods: in 1849, he was elected as a Deputy, and again, at the end of his life, he became interested in the "Manifesto of the Sixty" Paris workers, published in 1863. One cannot imagine Proudhon attending the meetings of the Paris branch of the International, though its French leaders did defend Proudhonian doctrines at the International Congresses and the largest single group in the Paris Commune of 1871 was Proudhonian. One Communard simply carried around an uncut copy of *On the Political Capacity of the Working Classes* as evidence of his own good faith in the workers' revolution. In the late 1860s Proudhonian often simply meant emphasizing economic forms of working-class organization as against purely political activity.

Under the Third Republic his name was associated with the non-Marxist socialist tradition, and his "peasant socialism"[38] was clearly well suited to a country which, until relatively recently, had a high proportion of its labor force engaged in agriculture (over 50 percent in 1870; 35 percent in 1930). Before the split between the French Socialist and Communist parties in 1920, both Proudhonian and Marxist ideas were combined, e.g. by Jean Jaurès, to produce a native form of French Socialism. Today cooperative ideas are often advocated as the most suitable alternative in French Africa to capitalism. Hard work, mutualism, a balance between agriculture and industry, and a suspicion of the power of the governing elite are the

---

in E. Laskine, *L'Internationale et le pangermanisme*, Paris, 1916. The First International broke up as a result of the split between those who tended to support Marx and the pro-French followers of Bakunin, who similarly charged that the International was subject to German domination.

[38] Cf. A. Berthod, *P. J. Proudhon et la propriété; un socialisme pour les paysans*, Paris, 1910.

noticeable Proudhonian elements of this African socialism.[39]

George Sorel claimed Proudhon for the French Syndicalists because Proudhon had argued that working-class
political action should be through mutualist associations
rather than political parties. Fernand Pelloutier's *Fédération des bourses du travail* tried to educate the French
working class along mutualist lines, arguing that the workers' organizations, the *syndicats*, were both a preparation
for the revolution and a pattern for the future organization of society. Léon Jouhaux, who from 1909 to 1947
was the General Secretary of the largest French Trade-
Union Confederation, the C.G.T., had been greatly influenced by this syndicalist element in Proudhon.[40] But
Proudhon would not have accepted the syndicalists'
view of the necessity for class hostility between the
bourgeoisie and the proletariat, although Sorel tried to
claim that Proudhon had believed in the class war.[41]
Proudhon's socialism was, rather, an alliance of the lesser
bourgeoisie, the industrial workers and the peasants, on
the grounds of a common equality of property, against
the growing wealth of the capitalist class. In his last book,
however, Proudhon went further and came closer to sin-

[39] See further P. Worsley, *The Third World*, London, 1964,
pp. 164–67; Mamadou Dia, *Réflexions sur l'économie de
l'Afrique noire*, Paris, 1960, pp. 59–67, and *Contribution à
l'étude du mouvement coopératif en Afrique noire*, Paris,
1958; R. Dumont, *False Start in Africa*, English translation,
London, 1966, passim; T. L. V. Blair, *The Land to Those
Who Work It*, New York, 1969.

[40] After the split in the C.G.T. of 1947 until his death in
1954 Jouhaux was the President of the French Economic
Council: see further on Proudhon and Jouhaux, J. E. S. Hay-
ward, *Private Interests and Public Policy. The Experience of
the French Economic and Social Council*, London and New
York, 1966, pp. 8–15.

[41] *Exégèses proudhoniennes*, in *Matériaux d'une théorie du
prolétariat*, Paris, 1921, p. 418.

gling out the working class as the leaders of such an alliance.[42]

It is nevertheless his defense of the small-property owner that provides the logic to Proudhon's writings. In this connection Proudhon's early notoriety as the author who had shown that "property is theft" is misleading. It was the absence of any link between owning the land and working it that Proudhon attacked in his *First Memoir on Property*. He criticized what he considered were the abuses of ownership, particularly the law of escheat and the renting of property. At first Proudhon argued that the only form of property ownership should be the right of "possession." By this he meant that the land should belong only to those who worked it, though he did allow the State the right to intervene to insure that the land was properly cultivated by its owners.

Later, Proudhon came to consider that liberty could be guaranteed only if property ownership was not subject to any limitation save that of size. This development can best be seen in his posthumously published *Theory of Property*, where Proudhon reverses his earlier preference for "possession" rather than "property" as a form of ownership, arguing instead that the individual must be absolutely sovereign over his own land. But right from the first, Proudhon argued in favor of the small farm, one just large enough to support a peasant family. His basic conviction was that the peasant wanted to be able to own the land he worked on, and to be free to pass it on to his children—in contrast to Bakunin, for example, who persuaded the First International to vote in favor of the abolition of the right of inheritance. In effect, Proudhon's writings on property were able to combine an attack on large-scale ownership, which gave his writings a revolutionary reputation, with a conservative defense of the small-peasant owner.

[42] Cf. below, pp. 175–78.

At the heart of all of Proudhon's writings on social questions there is this concern for the small-property holder. His proposals for monetary reform, his idea of a land bank, his mutual-insurance schemes, all reflected the ideals of the *petite-bourgeoisie*, their constant preoccupation with obtaining credit and their envy of the large-scale capitalist. Nor did Proudhon's support of agricultural co-operatives conflict with his views on property. Associations would be a way of instructing the peasants in new farming methods, and would enable them to afford co-operative buying of new machines. In this way the peasant farmers could prevent themselves from being driven off the land. But any such co-operation, in Proudhon's view, must be between independent producers. He strongly opposed any idea of the common ownership of land and he always defended hereditary property as one of the foundations of the family and of society.

To see Proudhon as a philosopher of the *petite-bourgeoisie* is to associate him with the long tradition of the discontent of the middleman and the small-peasant farmer. This has often been ill organized and has taken a number of different channels. During the French Revolution, for the most part, the Paris crowds who carried out the great "days" of the Revolution were composed of artisans, craftsmen, small shopkeepers and manufacturers, who worked, ate and slept alongside the few workers they employed. The social demand of these sans-culottes was not to abolish property but to extend it to all sections of society. They wanted equality; an end to, or at least a reduction of, the extremes of wealth and destitution. They were against commerce and against the owners of big capital in order to preserve the independence of their shops and ateliers.[43] By 1848 this was becoming increasingly less the case, and Proudhon's views on property,

[43] Cf. A. Soboul, *Les Sans-culottes parisiens en l'an II*, Paris, 1958, pp. 411–91.

which would have been shared by the avant-garde of the time of Robespierre, were not so clearly those of the burgeoning industrial proletariat of the latter half of the nineteenth century.

In North America it is the class background of the various populist movements, which have always had strong rural support. This "agrarian radicalism," as it has been called, is primarily opposed to big business and finance, and to the Government so far as it is seen to represent these interests against the small man. In England there are striking similarities between the Social Credit ideas of Major C. H. Douglas and the *"petit-bourgeois radicalism"* of Proudhon.[44] In France it was from the discontent of the *petite-bourgeoisie* that the nationalist *Action française* movement won its first considerable electoral support.[45] More recently this discontent has been expressed by the Poujadist movement, whose strength lay with the small shopkeepers and in rural areas where the owner-occupier farms were too small to be viable.[46] It is only by insisting on the extremes in Proudhon's thought, however, that he can be called a "harbinger of fascism."[47] For, in spite of the violence of his style,

[44] C. B. Macpherson, *Democracy in Alberta*, Toronto, 1953, p. 235. Cf. S. M. Lipset, *Agrarian Socialism*, Berkeley, 1950, pp. 3–19; Worsley, *op. cit.*, pp. 167–74.

[45] Cf. E. Weber, *The Nationalist Revival in France: 1905 –1914*, Berkeley, 1959, pp. 25, 62–70, 149–51; D. R. Watson, *The Nationalist Movement in Paris 1900–1906* in *The Right in France: 1890–1919*, ed. D. Schapiro, St. Antony's papers No. 13, London, 1962, pp. 68–82; R. Girardet, *Le Nationalisme français* (1871–1914), Paris, 1966, pp. 26–27. See also S. M. Lipset, *Political Man*, London and New York, 1960, Ch. 5.

[46] Cf. P. M. Williams, *Crisis and Compromise: Politics in the Fourth Republic*, London and New York, 1964, pp. 164–69. See further S. Hoffmann, *Le Movement Poujade*, Paris, 1956.

[47] By J. S. Schapiro in *Liberalism and the Challenge of Fascism: Social Forces in England and France, 1815–1870*, New York, 1949, p. 365. Henri Bachelin published a fascist study of Proudhon during the Vichy regime: *Les Précurseurs: P. J. Proudhon, socialiste national*, Paris 1941.

Proudhon hated all forms of militarism, and his mutualist and federalist ideas were intended as alternatives to the development of mass politics. Proudhon's etymological anarchism is closer to the French Radical tradition of the Third Republic than to attempts at "propaganda by the deed" or revolution by a General Strike. Proudhon's writings on the State have many similarities to Alain's *Elements of a Radical Doctrine*, with its suspicion of the State and its doctrine that the individual must constantly struggle to prevent authority from trampling his liberties.[48]

In true Radical fashion Proudhon temperamentally preferred to remain isolated. Like an Old Testament prophet, he proclaimed the truth as he saw it about a society he largely condemned. He was, as he claimed, an interpreter of his times, though from the standpoint of a particular class. The small-property owners and small employers who were threatened by the expansion of capitalist production on a scale they could not afford could hardly look to the collectivist socialists to defend their property. As the philosopher who expressed many of the aspirations of this class, Proudhon shared in the ambiguity of its social position, defending in the name of anarchism an individualistic notion of liberty while criticizing the new industrial capitalism in the name of social justice. The contradiction this entailed, and which Proudhon erected into the very principle of his thinking, is one reason for his sense of tragedy and for the mixing of passion and irony in his writings.

[48] Alain, *Éléments d'une doctrine radicale*, Paris, 1925; cf. A. Thibaudet, *Les Idées politiques de la France*, Paris, 1932, p. 171: "Radicalism cannot be explained without taking into account its Proudhono-Alainian element." Michel Crozier, *The Bureaucratic Phenomenon*, Chicago, 1964, pp. 213–69 interprets the whole French social system in terms of this anarchic individualism.

Selected Writings of
PIERRE-JOSEPH PROUDHON

PART ONE

Social Criticism and Social Order

I THE DIVISION OF LABOR

Let us imagine wealth as a mass that is maintained by a chemical force in a permanent state of composition into which new elements are constantly being introduced so as to combine in different proportions while remaining in accord with a fixed law. Value is the proportional relationship (the measure) of each of these elements to the whole.

Two things follow from this: first, that the economists were completely mistaken in trying to find a standard of value in wheat, money, rent, etc., as well as in concluding, when they had demonstrated that none of these things provided a standard of value, that value is not a rational thing and cannot be measured. Secondly, that the proportion of the different values may vary continually, while at the same time remaining subject to a law, whose determination is precisely the answer we require . . . .

I therefore postulate some force that in fixed proportions combines the elements of wealth and makes them into a homogeneous whole. If the constituent elements are not present in the required proportions, the combination will take place nevertheless, but instead of absorbing the whole substance it will reject part of it as useless. The internal movement producing the combination and determining the affinity of the various substances is, in society, exchange. Exchange considered here not only in its elementary form as between one man and another, but exchange considered as the fusion of all the values produced by private industry into one single social wealth. Finally, I call value the proportion in which each element contributes to the whole, and *non-value* the excess which remains after the combination has taken place, to the extent that this excess cannot be combined and exchanged if a certain quantity of other elements is added . . . .

This force, which Adam Smith extolled with such eloquence and which his successors have misunderstood, attributing equal importance to privilege, is LABOR. Labor varies in both quantity and quality from producer to producer. In this it is like all the great principles of nature and the most general laws, which are simple in their operation and formula but infinitely variable in the number of particular causes they may have and the endless varieties or forms they may take. It is labor, and labor alone, that produces all the elements of wealth and makes them combine, down to the very last molecule, following a variable but definite law of proportionality. And finally it is labor as a principle of life that activates the substance of wealth, *mens agitat molem*,[1] and determines its proportions.

> (1846)   *Econ. Contrads.* I, pp. 105–8

It is said that the capitalist pays the workers for their day's labor. But to be precise, what ought to be said is that the number of days he has paid for is equivalent to the number of laborers he has employed each day. This is by no means the same thing since he has paid nothing for the enormous collective force which results from the laborers' communal effort, or from the fact that they are all working at the same thing at the same time. Two hundred grenadiers set up the Luxor obelisk[2] in the space of a few hours. Does anyone suppose that one man could have managed it in two hundred days? Yet in the capitalist's reckoning the total wages would have been the same. Now, cultivating a wilderness, building a house, or run-

[1] "Mind activates matter."
[2] In the *Place de la Concorde*, Paris, erected in 1836.

ning a factory is like setting up an obelisk or moving a mountain. The smallest fortune, the most insignificant business concern, the most trifling industrial process demands the collaboration of such a wide variety of skills that no one man can suffice. It is astonishing that the economists have not noticed this fact. Let us therefore weigh up the balance between what the capitalist has received and what he has paid for . . . .

What is a man hoping to exploit when he hires out his services? It is the property owner's presumed need of him and will to employ him. Just as formerly the commoner owed the tenure of his land to the bounty and good pleasure of the feudal lord, so today the worker owes his labor to the good pleasure and needs of the employer and property owner. This is termed holding on sufferance. But this precarious condition is unjust since it implies inequality in bargaining. The worker's wages scarcely exceed his daily expenditure and in no way guarantee his next day's wages, while the capitalist is assured of independence and security in the future by the instrument the worker produces.

Now this fertile leaven, this constant source of life, this accumulation of capital and instrument of production is what the capitalist owes to the producer, but he never pays him for it. It is this fraudulent deprivation which causes the poverty of the worker, the opulence of the idle and the inequality of their conditions. And it is this, above all, which has so aptly been called the exploitation of man by man . . . .

The force of a thousand men working for twenty days is paid at the same rate as the force of one man working for fifty-five years, but the force of the thousand men achieves in twenty days what the force of one man's continuous effort could not achieve in a million centuries. Can we say, therefore, that such a basis of remuneration is just? I must repeat, no, we cannot. Even when you have repaid the force of each individual man, you have not repaid the collective force. Consequently there remains a collective property right that you have not rightfully acquired and that you therefore enjoy unjustly.

I admit that twenty days' wages may be enough to feed, lodge and clothe all these workers for twenty days. But when they have no more work after their time has expired, what will become of them if, while they have been working, they have been surrendering their produce to the owners by whom they are shortly to be abandoned? While the owner, who is more firmly established thanks to all that the workers have done, lives in security and has no more fears that he will be short of work or bread, the worker's only hope lies in the goodwill of this same owner, to whom he has sold and bound over his liberty. If therefore the property owner, complacently taking refuge in his affluence and his legal rights, refuses to employ the worker, how will the worker live? He has prepared an excellent piece of ground, but he will never sow it with seed. He has built a comfortable and magnificent house, but he will never live in it. He has produced everything, but he will enjoy nothing.

Through labor we are advancing toward equality, and each step we take brings us closer to it. If the strength, diligence and industry of workers were equal, it is evident that their fortunes would be equal too. In fact, if (as it is claimed and as I have agreed) the worker is the owner of the value he creates, it follows that:

1. The worker is gaining at the expense of the idle property owner.

2. Since all production is necessarily collective, the worker has the right to share in the products and profits in proportion to the amount of work he has contributed.

3. Since all accumulated capital is collective property, no one may be its exclusive owner.

These consequences are unavoidable and are sufficient

in themselves to upset our whole economy and to alter completely our institutions and laws.

                    (1840)   *Memoir* pp. 215–18

Whether all the parts of a watch are made by one and the same worker or by fifty different workers in no way affects the unity of the product. It will still be one single product. It is as if, instead of being made by one individual in successive stages, the different parts of the watch were made by one worker with fifty heads and a hundred arms. Thus the division of labor is synonymous with multiplying the number of workers. The division of labor and the collective force, or co-operative action, are two correlative facets of the same law. Now, according to whether one considers it in terms of the *product* or in terms of the *worker,* Adam Smith's principle produces different consequences.[3] Some, as I stated just now, constitute the science of production and circulation of wealth and others the science of *Organization,* which is the second branch of political economy . . . .

The division of labor presupposes diversity of talents and it produces exchange. The collection of individual forces is simply the general series of workers considered as one entity.

From this principle, demonstrated in the form of a serial equation, the following corollaries have been deduced:

1. Through the division of labor, which has become a collective force, the relation between the workers is naturally one of association and they are dependent upon each other.

2. Because they are partners and jointly responsible,

[3] Proudhon relates his discussion of the division of labor closely to that of Adam Smith in *The Wealth of Nations,* Bk. I, ch. 1.

the principle and even the possibility of competition between them is eliminated.

3. The collective force of a hundred workers is incomparably greater than that of one worker multiplied by a hundred. Since this force is not accounted for in the wages of a hundred individual workers there is a miscalculation [*erreur de compte*] operating today between workers and employers, and the laws of associations ought to be reformulated.

4. The most talented people, both in their development and in the use they make of their talents, are part of the collective force and are subject to the laws of solidarity in the same way as those who perform the least important functions. In addition, the former owe much more to society than do the latter. Thus there can be much less justification for claims to excessive salaries.

5. Workers' wages are in fact simply given in exchange for their services. Thus equality of functions which are associated should result in equal conditions for all workers, at least insofar as this is possible given the physical, intellectual and moral anomalies that afflict the human race. These anomalies must gradually be eliminated through the principles of the division of labor and the collective force, the theory of serial law, and reforms in education and hygiene.

6. Any other basis for the distribution of instruments of labor and the sharing of products is iniquitous usurpation.

The only reply that has been made to these different formulae, which provide the basis for a new system of jurisprudence, has been to dismiss the case. This is either because the privileged classes have a vested interest in preserving the *status quo*, or because of the absence of any theory of organization which would enable the things pointed out by the critics to be rectified. In order to put things right the proletariat is called upon to provide a pattern for order, that is to say, to create the very science of Economics.

(1843) *Creation* pp. 301–2

Let us take the case of the farmer. Before the onset of winter he plows the fields and sows wheat and rye. In the spring he plants maize, potatoes, hemp and coleseed. In summer he makes hay and harvests, while in the autumn he is busy with the wine harvest. Then he stores and conserves his crops. All the while he has been carrying out numerous other ancillary tasks. Each of these successive operations forms a portion of the process of farming and it takes a whole year to complete and assess the farmer's total labor . . . .

All the most ingenious, intricate and complex of man's tasks are necessarily performed in infinitely small stages. But when they are linked together, these stages in the end combine to form a whole, composite series. Now, immobilizing the worker within one infinitely small area of production constitutes what has been termed the division of labor. I maintain that this immobility is the result of a confusion and is a consequence of the oversimplified application of the right of property, which everything is helping to abolish . . . .

One quite frequently meets men of real ability and highly developed talent who, for the same wage, prefer to do the simplest and most monotonous jobs because they want to reserve their intellectual effort for unrestricted creative activities, for which they do not expect to receive payment. In such instances the division of labor, which is harmful neither to society nor to the individual if it is capably managed and co-ordinated, has no disadvantages. One day perhaps this may well come to be the way in which we all live. When a man has reached his full potential in youth, has thoroughly explored his specialized sphere of activity, and has been in a position to command and instruct others, he likes, when the time comes, to withdraw into himself and have time to reflect. Then, providing he is assured a daily wage, content that he has proved himself, he leaves it to others to carry out great plans and fill dazzling posts, and gives himself up to the musings of his heart, which the regularity of the subdivision of labor serves only to encourage.

(1843)   *Creation* pp. 334–38

II   ECONOMICS AND JUSTICE

My father, who was a simple man, could never get it into his head that the society he lived in was based on antagonism, that the well-being each industrialist aims at is booty as much as it is the product of labor, and that consequently the market price of a product is not measured in terms of its cost price, but in terms of what the needs of the public, their buying power, the state of competition and so on allow the industrialist to extort. My father used to add up his expenses, add so much for his labor and say: "My price is such and such." He would listen to no objections and so he brought about his own ruin. Even before I was twelve, when I was working as a cellar-boy, I began to reflect on my father's methods of conducting business and on the remarks made by his friends. Without knowing it I was reasoning about *supply* and *demand* and *net earnings,* like Pascal with his *rounds* and *bars* reasoning about geometry.[4] I was perfectly well aware that my father's method was honest and straight, but I was nonetheless aware of the risks it entailed. My

[4] At the age of twelve Pascal, who up to then had been taught no mathematics, was discovered by his father trying to prove a theorem in geometry and calling circles "rounds" and straight lines "bars."

conscience approved of my father's course of action but
desire for our security attracted me toward the other.
This posed something of a riddle for me since it was contrary to Christian doctrine, and solving it would have
meant destroying my religious beliefs . . . .

Nothing, I replied, has proved that conflicting wills
and interests cannot be balanced so as to produce peace,
lasting peace, and wealth as a condition for all men.
There is nothing to prove that vice and crime, which are
taken to be the cause of poverty and antagonism, are
not in fact caused by poverty and antagonism: Catholic
doctrine presents poverty and antagonism as being the
punishment for vice and crime. What we must do is discover some principle of harmony, equipoise and equilibrium.

(1858)   *Justice* II, pp. 5–6

It is evident everywhere that immorality increases in
proportion to economic progress, so that society seems to
be based on the fatal, indissoluble dualism of *wealth* and
poverty, improvement and *corruption*. Since the economists also demonstrate that Justice is itself an economic
force, that wherever it is violated by servitude, despotism,
lack of security, etc., production is affected, wealth decreases and barbarity increases, it follows that political
economy, that is to say the whole of society, is a network
of contradictions. This is something which Rossi[5] did
not see, or which perhaps he did not dare to point out.

[5] P. L. E. Rossi, 1787–1848, an Italian economist who succeeded J. B. Say as professor at the *Collège de France* in
1833. Proudhon was struck, like other socialists of his time, by
the implication of classical economics that wealth depended
on poverty. Thus Proudhon was concerned with how economics and justice could be reconciled. Rossi suggested in
his Courses that the conclusions of economics when applied to
society needed supplementing by political and moral considerations.

You will find this antinomy explained at length in my *System of Economic Contradictions*. But what is the official, expert view of it?

Some who are extremist disciples of Malthus, speak out boldly against Justice. First and foremost, and at any price, they demand wealth, of which they hope to have their share. They attach little value to the life, liberty and intelligence of the masses. On the pretext that it is a law of economics and the will of destiny, they remorselessly sacrifice humanity to Mammon. This is what has distinguished the *economist* school in its struggle against socialism. May this go down in history as its crime and its shame.

Others draw back in alarm before the developments of economics and look back in anguish to the days when industry was simple and spinning was done in the home, to the days of the communal bakehouse. Thus they retreat into the past.

I think that here, too, I have been the first person with a full understanding of the situation who has dared to say that Justice and economics ought not to restrict each other or make trivial concessions. This would merely be detrimental to both, and useless. They ought to be systematically interwoven, Justice serving as a law for economics. Thus, instead of restraining the economic forces, whose distorted growth is killing us, we ought to make them BALANCE each other by virtue of a little-known and even less well-understood principle: namely, that opposites should not destroy but should compensate each other, precisely because they are opposites.

I would like to term this the application of Justice to political economy, in the same way as Descartes called his analysis the application of algebra to geometry. This, says Rossi, is the new science, the true science of society.

(1865) *Justice* II, pp. 59–61

Since the law of nature as well as of Justice is equality, and since the aims of both are identical, economists and statesmen no longer have to decide whether economics should be sacrificed to Justice, or Justice to economics. They have to discover how best to exploit the physical, intellectual and economic forces that human intelligence is perpetually discovering in order to restore the social equilibrium, which is momentarily upset by the contingencies of climate, population growth, education, illness and all like accidents of *force-majeure*.

One man, for example, is bigger and stronger than another. One is successful in agriculture, another in industry or shipping. One is able to take in a vast complex of events and ideas at a glance. Another is unequaled in a more limited sphere. In all these cases certain compensations must be made for an equalizing process to be operated that would give rise to stimulating competition and friendly rivalry. The way that man is constituted and the way that industry is divided provides unlimited sources for checking manifestations of superiority and for constantly creating new means of maintaining equality between the unknown forces of nature and society.

This then is the radical and forever insurmountable difference which separates Christian and Malthusian economics, which are both materialistic and mystical, from revolutionary economics.

The first, which bases its judgment on the phenomena of chance and anomaly, does not hesitate to declare that men are by nature unequal. Then, without bothering to compare the kinds of work men do or to examine the results of their labors, their education and the effects of the separation of employment—and taking good care not to look too closely at each man's share of the collective product, nor to compare what he receives with what he contributes—they conclude that this so-called inequality justifies the privileges of exploitation and property-owning.

The Revolution, on the other hand, starts with the assumption that equality is the law of nature and that men are naturally equal. If it turns out in practice that some are less equal, it is because they have not wanted, or have not known how, to make full use of their possibilities. The Revolution considers that the hypothesis that men are unequal is an unfounded insult which is daily disproved by the progress of science and industry. It devotes all its energy to trying to redress the balance, tipped by prejudice, by means of legislation and greater and greater equality of services and wages. This is why it declares that all men *have equal rights* and are equal before the law. On the one hand it wants all industries, professions, functions, arts, sciences and trades to be considered as equally noble and worthy of merit. On the other it wants all parties in any litigation and competition to be treated equally, except when there is a difference in value between products and services. And so that equal Justice for all may become increasingly widespread in society, it wants all citizens to enjoy equal opportunities for development and action.

(1858)   *Justice* II, pp. 69–70

How could any virtue or good faith survive in a society whose basic maxim is that economics has nothing to do with justice, that it is totally separate from it, that the idea of economic Justice is an economic utopia and that thus the existing economic order (so it is claimed) is not based on any judicial considerations? In a society where men can promise each other anything they like, but where as a result of their economic relations they owe each other absolutely nothing in reality, and where in consequence, since every man is entitled to pursue his own interest to the exclusion of others, friend could legitimately, logically and scientifically ruin friend, or son abandon father and mother, or worker betray his employer, etc. How could there be any respect for property in such a system? What power could there be in association, what respect for authority, what faith in law, what dignity in man?

(1865)   *Pol. Cap.* p. 228

What then, in more explicit terms, is political economy? What is socialism?

Political economy is the sum of observations made to date about the phenomena of the production and distribution of wealth, that is to say about the most general, spontaneous and, consequently, most authentic forms of labor and exchange.

The economists have classified these observations as well as they can. They have described the phenomena and noted their anomalies and relationships. They have noticed in a number of circumstances the presence of a certain necessity which has made them speak of *laws*. This body of knowledge, based on what one might call the simplest phenomena of society, constitutes political economy . . . .

Socialism, which, like the god Vishnu, is forever dying and forever being born anew, has in the space of the last twenty years or so reached its ten-thousandth incarnation in the shape of five or six prophets. Socialism asserts that the present constitution of society, and consequently of all previous societies, is anomalous.

It claims and proves that civilized order is artificial, contradictory and ineffective, and that of itself it engenders oppression, poverty and crime. It accuses, not to say vilifies, the whole past life of organized society and pushes forward with all its might toward the remolding of habits and institutions.

Socialism concludes by declaring that political economy is based on a false hypothesis and that it is a system of sophistry invented to abet the exploitation of the greatest

c

number by the smallest. Applying the maxim *a fructibus cognoscetis*,[6] it completes its demonstration of the powerlessness and emptiness of political economy by presenting the canvas of human calamities, for which socialism holds political economy responsible.

But if political economy is false, so is jurisprudence, which in all countries is the science of laws and customs. For it is founded on the distinction between mine and thine and presupposes the legitimacy of the facts that political economy describes and classifies. The theories of public and international law, together with all the varieties of representative government, must likewise be false, since they are based on the principle of individual ownership of property and the absolute sovereignty of the will of individuals.

Socialism accepts all these consequences. It sees political economy, which some regard as the physiology of wealth, as being simply organized theft and poverty, just as it sees jurisprudence, which the lawyers have adorned with the title of codified reason, as being simply a compilation of legal and official titles for robbery, that is, for property. In the socialists' view these two so-called sciences, political economy and law, considered in relation to each other, form a complete theory of injustice and discord. Moving from destructive criticism to positive suggestion, socialism proposes the principle of association instead of that of property, and undertakes to reconstruct the economics of society[7] from top to bottom.

[6] "By their fruits ye shall know them."

[7] Here and elsewhere Proudhon uses the term *l'économie sociale*, social economy, in contrast to *l'économie politique*, political economy. By this term Proudhon meant a new science of the economy of society that would be other than *laissez-faire* capitalism and based on justice and the rights of the individual. A possible translation would be "socialist economics," except that Proudhon is here arguing that socialism is only a stage, the antithesis of capitalism, of which the final synthesis

That is to say, socialism undertakes to re-create a new law, a new political system, and institutions and morals which differ in every possible way from the old forms.

Thus there is a sharply defined dividing line between socialism and political economy. The hostility between the two is open.

Political economy leans toward consecrating egoism; socialism leans toward putting the community before everything else . . . .

Now modern criticism[8] has shown that in a conflict of this kind the truth is not to be found by excluding one of the opposite terms, but only by reconciling them. It is, I repeat, a known scientific fact that all antagonisms, whether in nature or in ideas, become resolved in a more general term or complex formula which reconciles the opposing sides by, so to speak, assimilating them both. Could not we therefore, who are men of common sense, while we are awaiting the solution the future will doubtless bring, prepare ourselves for this great change by analyzing the opposing forces and looking at their positive and negative qualities? Such a task, carried out carefully and conscientiously, even if it does not lead straight to the solution, would at least have the inestimable advantage of revealing the nature of the problem, and in so doing, of putting us on our guard against all utopias.

(1846)   *Econ. Contrads.* I, pp. 67–72

If a truly social economics is still today more of a tentative reaching toward the future than a knowledge of reality as it is, we must also recognize that the elements of this branch of study are all to be found in political economy. I think I am expressing the general feeling in

is "mutualism," i.e. a society founded on the principles of association and equal exchange.

[8] Proudhon is here referring to his recent studies of the German philosophers; cf. *Introduction,* pp. 18–19 above.

saying that this opinion is now held by most people. It is true that few people defend the present state of affairs, but the distaste for utopias is no less widespread, and it is generally accepted that the truth is to be found in some formula which would reconcile the two terms: CONSERVATION and PROGRESSION.

(1846)   *Econ. Contrads.* I, p. 86

Socialism is right to protest against political economy and say that it is simply an unthinking mechanism, and political economy is right to say that socialism is merely an unrealistic utopia which cannot possibly come into being. But since each in turn is denying something, socialism humanity's past experience and political economy humanity's reason, both are inadequate statements about the truth of human life.

Social science is the marriage of reason and social practices. While our former teachers had only rare glimpses of this science, it will be given to us in this century to contemplate it in all its splendor and sublime harmony!

(1846)   *Econ. Contrads.* II, p. 391

III MUTUALISM

If I am not much mistaken, the reader must be convinced of at least one thing, namely: that the truth about society lies neither in utopias nor in blind routine. Political economy is not the science of society, but it contains the elements of this science just as chaos before creation contained the elements of the universe; in order to arrive at the definitive organization which seems to be the destiny of our species on earth, all we have to do is to arrange all our contradictions in the form of a general equation.

But what form will this equation take?

We are already beginning to glimpse it. It must be based on a law of *exchange*, a theory of MUTUALITY, a system of guarantees that resolves the old forms of our civil and commercially based societies and satisfies all the conditions of efficiency, progress and justice pointed out by the critics. It will be a society that is not based on convention, but on reality; a society that converts the division of labor into a scientific instrument; a society that stops men from being the slaves of machines and foresees the crises that these will cause. It will make competition profitable and transform monopoly into a guarantee of security for all. Through the energy of its principle, instead of asking the capitalist for credit and the State for protection, it will make both capital and the State subordinate to labor. Through the genuine nature of exchange it will create true solidarity between peoples. It will, without prohibiting individual initiative or domestic thrift, always restore to the community the wealth that has been privately appropriated. It will be a society that will, through the movement of the *outlay* and the *return* of capital, insure the political and industrial equality of its citizens, and through a vast system of public education bring about equality in functions and aptitudes through constantly raising their level. Through justice, prosperity and virtue it will bring a renewal of human consciousness and insure harmony and equilibrium between the generations. In short it will be a society which, since it is based on both an organized structure and on the possibility of change, will be more than provisional; it will guarantee everything while pledging nothing ...

The theory of *mutuality*, or *mutuum*, that is to say exchange in kind, of which the simplest form is the loan for consumption,[9] where the collective body is concerned, is

---

[9] A *loan for consumption* is an agreement whereby one person delivers to another a certain quantity of things to be con-

the synthesis of the notions of private property and collective ownership. This synthesis is as old as its constituent parts since it merely means that society is returning, through a maze of inventions and systems, to its primitive practices as a result of a six-thousand-year-long meditation on the fundamental proposition that A = A.

(1846)   *Econ. Contrads.* I, pp. 410–11

The principle of mutualism[10] was first expressed with any philosophical sophistication and in a spirit of reform in the famous maxim all the sages have repeated, which our Constitutions of the Year II and of the Year III[11] included in the *Declaration of the Rights and Duties of Man and of the Citizen:*

Do not do unto others as you would not have them do unto you. Always do unto others as you would they should do unto you . . . .

First, how and under what influence did the idea of mutualism take hold of people's minds?

We have already looked at the way in which the Luxembourg school[12] sees the relation of man and the citizen

---

sumed, under the obligation, by the borrower, of returning as many things of the same kind and quality.

[10] While Proudhon was working in Lyon as a clerk from 1843–47, he came into contact with the Mutualists. This was a secret society among Lyon factory workers, who were at this time the most revolutionary in France. Proudhon saw in them an emphasis on economic and social change, as opposed to the Republican and Jacobin idealization of political revolution. For this reason he seems to have used the name of this society to summarize his own ideas on social organization.

[11] That is, the Jacobin Constitution of 1793 and the 1795 Constitution that founded the Directory.

[12] Proudhon is referring to Louis Blanc and the Luxembourg Commission of 1848, which for a short while established national workshops for unemployed Parisians. Shortly after the failure of this Commission, Blanc defended himself against

to society and to the State. According to them, the relation is one of subordination. An authoritarian and communist organization follows from this.

In opposition to this idea of government is that of the defenders of individual liberty. According to them, society must be thought of not as a hierarchical system of functions and faculties, but as a system of free forces balancing each other; a system in which all individuals are guaranteed the same rights provided they perform the same duties, one in which they will receive the same benefits in return for the same services rendered. This system is thus essentially egalitarian and liberal and precludes all notion of fortune, rank or class. Now this is how these anti-authoritarians or liberals conclude their argument.

They maintain that since human nature is the most elevated expression not to say the embodiment of universal Justice, man as citizen derives his rights from the dignity of his nature. Similarly, he will later gain well-being directly from his personal labor and the good use he makes of his faculties, as well as respect from the free exercise of his talents and virtues. They say therefore that the State is simply the product of the freely consented union formed by equal, independent subjects, all of whom alike are lawmakers. Thus the State represents only group interests, and any debate between Power and the citizen is really only a debate between citizens. Accordingly, the only prerogative in society is liberty, the only supreme force, Law. Authority and charity, they say, have served their time. What we want instead is justice.

From these premises, which are radically opposed to those of the Luxembourg Commission, they conclude in favor of an organization based on the widest possible application of the mutualist principle. Its law, they say, is service for service, product for product, loan for loan, in-

his critics (including Proudhon) by arguing that he had never intended the State to run his co-operative factories, only to help in starting them.

surance for insurance, credit for credit, security for security, guarantee for guarantee. It is the ancient law of
retaliation, *an eye for an eye, a tooth for a tooth, a life
for a life,* as it were turned upside down and transferred
from criminal law and the vile practices of the vendetta
to economic law, to the tasks of labor and to the good
offices of free fraternity. On it depend all the mutualist
institutions: mutual insurance, mutual credit, mutual aid,
mutual education; reciprocal guarantees of openings, exchanges and labor for good quality and fairly priced
goods, etc. This is what the principle of mutualism claims
to use, with the aid of certain institutions, as the foundation of the State, the law of the State, and I will even
go as far as to say as a kind of religion of the State, which
will be just as easy (in practice) as it is advantageous. It
demands no police force, no repression or restrictions,
and can never be a cause of disappointment or ruin for
anyone.

In this system the laborer is no longer a serf of the
State, swamped by the ocean of the community. He is a
free man, truly his own master, who acts on his own initiative and is personally responsible. He knows that he will
obtain just and sufficient payment for his products and
services, and that his fellow citizens will give him absolute
loyalty and complete guarantees for all the consumer
goods he might need. The State or government is no
longer sovereign. Authority is no longer the antithesis of
liberty, and State, government, power, authority, etc., are
only expressions that designate liberty in a different way.
They are general formulae borrowed from outmoded
speech which in certain cases signify the sum, the union,
the identity and the solidarity of individual interests.

From then on there is no need to ask (as there is in the
bourgeois system or that of the Luxembourg Commission)
whether the State, the government or the community
must govern the individual or be subject to him, whether
the prince is above the citizen or the citizen above the

prince, or whether authority is the master or *servant* of liberty, for all these questions are meaningless. Government, authority, the State, communities, corporations, classes, companies, cities, families, citizens—in short, groups and individuals, corporate bodies and persons, are all equal before the law. It alone, sometimes through the agency of the one and sometimes through the offices of the other, reigns, judges and governs: *Despotes ho nomos.*[13]

(1865)   *Pol. Cap.* pp. 120, 124–26

What was the Luxembourg Commission's intention concerning workers' associations? It was to replace capitalist associations by workers' unions and State subsidies; that is to say, to fight against free industry and trade by centralizing business, massing workers together and having bigger capital funds. The two or three thousand presently licensed firms in Paris would be replaced by a hundred or so large associations representing the various branches of industry and trade associations in which the working population would be regimented and subjected once and for all to the State's policy of capital. How could this be profitable to liberty, public happiness or civilization? It could not be. We would simply have exchanged our present chains for others. Furthermore—and this is sadder still, since it indicates the sterility of lawmakers, industrialists and reformers—society would not have advanced a single step. We would still be subject to the same economic arbitrariness, not to say fatalism . . . .

Mutualism is already beginning to appear as the *Deus ex machina*. We must therefore discover what it can teach us. To start with we must note that it is not the same thing as association . . . .

[13] "Law is the ruler."

c*

While we are considering association, let us note that mutualism intends men to associate only insofar as this is required by the demands of production, the cheapness of goods, the needs of consumption and the security of the producers themselves, i.e. in those cases where it is not possible for the public to rely on private industry, nor for private industry to accept the responsibility and risks involved in running the concerns on their own. Thus no systematized outlook, ambitious calculation, party spirit or vain sentimentality unites the persons concerned. It is the very nature of things; because they are acting in accordance with the very nature of things when they associate in this way, they can preserve their liberty without being any the less in an association . . . .

There is undoubtedly a case for association in the large-scale manufacturing, extractive, metallurgical and shipping industries. No one now disputes this. If we are considering one of the large enterprises that are in effect public services, such as railways, loan societies and docks, by the law of mutualism all these services, since they entail no capital profit, should be provided for the public at prices equivalent to the cost of development and maintenance. It is also evident that a guarantee of proper performance and low prices cannot be given either by companies holding a monopoly, or by State-run concerns that operate in the name of the State and for the State. This guarantee can be given only by free members of an association who have obligations both to the public, through the contract of mutuality, and to each other, through the normal contract of association.

What is the position if we think of the thousands of crafts and trades proliferating in the towns and even in the rural areas? For these I do not think association offers any advantages; all the more so since any benefits that might follow are already assured by the network of reciprocal guarantees, mutual credit and insurance, market control, etc., etc. I would add that when these guarantees have been made, it is safer for the public, in the cases I have mentioned, to deal with a single contractor than with a company.

(1865)   *Pol. Cap.* pp. 187–91

The particular aim of a mutualist society may be to develop one industry. But by virtue of the mutualist principle it tends to draw into its system of guarantees, first those industries with which it is in direct contact, and then those that are more distant. Seen in this way, clearly the mutualist association is unlimited in scope and may be increased in size indefinitely.

(1865)   *Pol. Cap.* p. 114

The aim of industrial and agricultural co-operatives, including workers' associations where these can usefully be formed, is not to substitute collectivities for individual enterprise, as was foolishly preached in 1848.[14] It is to secure for all small and medium-sized industrial entrepreneurs, as well as for small-property owners, the benefit of discoveries, machines, improvements and processes which would otherwise be beyond the reach of modest firms and fortunes.

(1863–64)   *Property* p. 183

Mutualism and Equality

In democratizing us, revolution has launched us on the path of industrial democracy. This is the first and very big step it has made us take. Another idea has resulted from this, namely the fixing of labor and wages . . . .

[14] An attack on the utopian ideas of his fellow socialists, especially the Fourierists, and probably Louis Blanc and the Luxembourg Commission: cf. footnote twelve above, p. 58.

Since we are living in a democracy and all enjoy the same rights, and since the law accords us all equal favor and consideration, I conclude that, when business is our concern, all questions of precedence must be put aside and we must consider only the intrinsic value of labor.

Utility equals utility.

Function equals function.

Service pays for service.

One day's work equals another day's work.

All products will be paid for by products that have cost the same in effort and expense.

If in a transaction of this kind any preference were to be given, it would not be to the brilliant, agreeable, honorific functions coveted by all, but, as Fourier said, to laborious tasks that shock our sensibilities and are an offense to man's self-esteem. Should it suit a rich man's whim to employ me as his personal valet, I would say to myself: "No job is stupid, there are only stupid people. Cares that are given to the human person are more than useful tasks, they are acts of charity that place the person who performs them above the person who receives them. Therefore, since I have no intention of being humiliated, I will place a condition upon my service: the man who wishes to employ me as a servant must pay me fifty per cent of his income. Without this we are going beyond the bounds of fraternity, equality and mutuality. I would even go so far as to say that we are going beyond the bounds of justice and morality. We are no longer democrats; we have become a society of valets and aristocrats."

But, you will say, it is not true that function equals function, that one service repays another and that the day's labor of one man equals that of another. Universal consciousness protests against this and declares that your mutuality would be an iniquity. Whether we like it or not, we must therefore maintain the law of supply and demand, tempered in its ruthless, false elements by education and philanthropy.

I must confess that I would almost prefer people to maintain that industrial workers, public servants, scholars, traders, workers, peasants—in a word, all those who labor, produce and are of use—can be compared with animals of different, unequal species between which no comparisons may be made. How can one compare the dignity of the beast of burden with that of man; what common measure is there between the bondage of the first and the noble, free action of the second? ... This is how the theorizers who support the theory of inequality argue. To them there is a greater difference between one man and another than there is between a man and a horse. They conclude from this that it is not only the products of human labor that are incommensurable, but that men themselves, in spite of anything that may have been written, are of unequal dignity and consequently of unequal rights, and that anything which is done to make them equal will be upset by the nature of things. This innate inequality between persons, they say, contains the principle of the inequality of ranks, conditions and fortunes . . . .

Society must be thought of as a giant with a thousand arms, who carries on all industries and simultaneously produces all forms of wealth. Society is animated by a single consciousness, a single mind and a single will, and the unity and oneness of its person is revealed in the co-ordination of its spheres of activity. Whatever it undertakes it always remains itself, as admirable and worthy in seeing to the smallest details as in the most amazingly complex operations. In all circumstances this prodigious being remains true to itself, and one may say that each moment of its existence is equally productive.

You persist and say: "Even if all the individuals who go to make up society are granted the same moral dignity, they will nevertheless, as far as their faculties are concerned, be unequal in relation to each other, and this is enough to ruin democracy, to whose laws they are supposedly subject."

To be sure, the individuals who make up society are unequal as far as faculties are concerned, in the same way as they are equal in dignity. What must we conclude from this? Only one thing: namely, that being certain of our equality, we must to the best of our ability, size up our inequalities.

Thus, save for the human personality, which we proclaim inviolable, and save for man's moral being and anything pertaining to consciousness, we must study both the natural limitations and the productive capacities of the man of action, or laborer. Now at first glance we perceive this very important fact: even if human faculties are unequal in different people, these differences of greater and lesser do not go on to infinity but remain within fairly restricted limits. Just as in physics it is impossible to reach extreme degrees of either heat or cold, our thermometers oscillating a little above or below a mean that is very improperly termed zero, so it is impossible to determine maximum and minimum limits to intelligence and strength, either in men or in beasts or in the Creator of the world. All we can do where the mind is concerned, for example, is mark degrees, which are necessarily arbitrary, above and below an agreed fixed point we will call *common sense*. As for strength, we can agree upon a metric unit, let us say horse power, and then count each man's units and fractions of units to measure his strength.

As in the case of the thermometer, therefore, we will have both *extremes* and a *mean* in our measurements of intelligence and strength. The mean is the point which the majority of people will reach. Those who go to the extremes above it or below it will be very rare. I said a moment ago that the distance between the two extremes is quite small; in fact anyone who had enough strength for two or three average men would be a veritable Hercules, and anyone who was *intelligent enough for four* would be a demigod. The conditions of life and nature must also be added to the limits imposed on human faculties. The *maximum* length of life is seventy to eighty years, and from these we must subtract the periods of childhood, education, retirement and senility.

There are twenty-four hours in a day for everyone. Of these, according to circumstances, from nine to eighteen may be spent in labor. Similarly, there is one day of rest in each week. Although there are three hundred and sixty-five days in the year, scarcely three hundred are devoted to labor. It is clear that even if the faculties for industry are unequal, this inequality will not prevent the whole from being very much on the same level. It is like a harvest field stretching as a smooth plain to the horizon, although taken individually the separate heads of corn are not of the same height.

In the light of these observations we may define a day's labor. In all industries and occupations it consists of the services or things of value that the man of average strength, intelligence and age—taking into account his situation and abilities—can produce in a given time: that is to say, ten, twelve or fifteen hours for those activities in which labor may be estimated in days, or a week, a month, a season or a year for those activities requiring a greater length of time.

Since children, women, old men, valetudinarians and sickly people cannot usually equal the average of the able-bodied, their day's work will be only a fraction of the official, normal, legal day that is the standard measure. I would say the same for the day's labor of the worker in a highly subdivided task, since his work is purely mechanical, more a matter of routine than intelligence, and cannot be compared to the labor of a truly industrial worker.

On the other hand, and by the same token, the above-average worker who thinks and works more rapidly and does more work of better quality than another—in particular, a worker who combines superior performance with a genius for directing and a capacity for organizing—will go beyond the normal average and will accordingly receive higher wages. He may earn one and a half, two, three days' wages or even more. Thus the rights of strength, talent and even character, as well as those of labor, are taken into account. If justice makes no distinctions between persons, neither does it overlook any capacity . . . .

But I repeat that if this arrangement is to be operable, a considerable amount of good faith must be present when labor, services and products are assessed. The working population must reach this degree of industrial and economic morality. Everyone must accept the justice that will be meted out without any consideration for the claims of vanity and personality, title, rank, precedent, honorary distinctions, fame—in short, of public consideration. Only the usefulness, quality and expenses of the product must be taken into account.

This system of comparing is, I maintain, eminently practical, and it is our duty to do everything we can to bring it into being. It precludes fraud, overcharging, charlatanism, sinecures, exploitation and oppression. But I must add that it cannot be treated as a domestic affair, a family virtue or a private moral act. The evaluation of labor and the repeated assessment of values is society's fundamental problem and it can be solved only by the collective will and the powers of the community.

(1865)   *Pol. Cap.* pp. 143, 146–50

The first consequence of rent, bonuses, tithes, interest, bribery, dividends, profits and the rest is that, by making universal competition impossible, it destroys the possibility of equal wages for different professions and social functions. The division of workers into two classes, laboring and skilled, managers and managed, is both irrational and unjust. Inequality of payment for different social functions is unjust because the functions are equally useful and we are all involved in the processes of production as a result of the division of these functions. No one can say that he produces goods by himself. The smith, the tailor, the shoemaker, etc., etc., all play their part with the farmer in tilling the soil, just as the farmer plays his part in the making of their products. The unskilled engineering worker plays his part in the work of the engineer just as the engineer does in his.

When I affirmed in my *First Memoir* that for equal work there ought to be equal pay in all types of employment, I omitted to say two things. (I rectified these omissions in my *Second Memoir* (1841), in *A Warning to Property Owners* (1842) and in *The Creation of Order in Humanity* (1843).) These were, first, that work is measured by multiplying time and effort, and second, that the wages of the worker must include neither the cost of his education and his self-improvement as an unpaid apprentice, nor his insurance premium against risks, since these vary considerably in different types of employment . . . .

When a worker includes in his apparent wages an insurance premium against the special risks of his job, it is in fact the consumer of his product who pays it. By exchanging goods for goods, or in more general terms, services for services, everybody is insured by everybody else against their respective risks, and since those who run the greatest risks receive the highest profits, it can be said that the aim of a universal society or association of workers is to institute equality of payment for all. If all *aubaines*[15]

15 Proudhon's account of some current usages of this term, quoting from his 1840 *Memoir,* is that *aubaine* is "called by different names according to its source: *rent,* for land, houses and movable property; *dividend,* for investments; *interest,* for money; *return, gain* or *profit* (none of which must be confused with wages or the legitimate price of labor) for business transactions": *Property,* p. 20.

are eliminated and if all premiums are paid to mutual insurance societies, then, without the assistance of charity (which is always inadequate because it is a graft on the social organism) there will be equality of payment in all types of employment. And if there is not, given these conditions, then the premiums have been miscalculated. If statistics are worked out on the basis I have indicated, it will not be long before the necessary adjustments are made. There will probably never be such a thing as absolute equality, but by a series of ever-decreasing adjustments it will be approached little by little, and approximate equality will soon be an established fact.

(1863–64)   *Property* pp. 21–24

The advocates of mutualism are as familiar as anyone with the laws of *supply* and *demand* and they will be careful not to infringe them. Detailed and frequently reviewed statistics, precise information about needs and living standards, an honest breakdown of cost prices, the foreseeing of all eventualities, the fixing after amicable discussion of a *maximum* and *minimum* profit margin, taking into account the risks involved, the organizing of regulating societies: these things, roughly speaking, constitute all the measures by means of which they hope to regulate the market. There will be as much liberty as you like, but more important than liberty are sincerity, reciprocity and enlightenment for all. Granted these circumstances, may the most diligent and the most upright have the largest clientele. This is their motto. Can anyone believe that after a few years of these reforms our commercial practices will not be completely altered, greatly increasing public happiness?

(1865)   *Pol. Cap.* p. 155

IV THE ORGANIZATION OF CREDIT

In what condition can a country provide food for the largest number of inhabitants and assure them the greatest possible well-being? Do you know the answer to this question, honest wage-owners, you who will never own an inch of land and who applaud the word *free-trade* in the same way as you do the word nationality? Have you even given the matter any thought?

The reply is simple, and when you hear it you will not for a moment doubt its validity: *it is when all people are owners of property that fortunes are most equal and there is work for everyone* . . . .

In short, a peasant family of four or five will live comfortably on a patrimony of some five hectares. This will provide, over and above taxes payable to the State, for additional industrial commodities, such as sheets, linen, edge tools, furniture, pottery and so on, which constitute an agricultural household. These, together with taxes, will make up one third of their consumption.

The population of France under this system of small-property owning could be of the order of nine million agricultural and wine-growing families, etc., making up a total of forty million inhabitants plus a third as many again for industrial workers, public servants, the army etc., say 13,500,000, making a total of 53,500,000 persons for the whole of France. Many people claim that France could in fact support twice this number.

How short of this figure is the present population of the Empire? It is about sixteen million short.[16]

What is the cause of this gap? I pointed out the cause

[16] The population of France at this time was around thirty-six million people.

just now. It is that property owners are in the minority, that fortunes are far from being equal, and that too many people are not working or are engaged in work of an unproductive kind. The cause is large-scale competition, large-scale industry, large-scale banks, large-scale companies, large-scale speculation and large-scale property; in a word, it is capitalist, commercial, industrial, property-based FEUDALISM,[17] which we allow to develop freely at the expense of the middle and laboring classes, and which at the moment the institution of free trade is trying to spread all over Europe and the globe.

(1865)   *Pol. Cap.* pp. 363–65

What is the aim, for example, of our large capitalist associations organized in the spirit of commercial and industrial feudalism? Their aim is the monopolizing of production, exchange and profits. To this end they try to group the most diverse specialized activities under one management and to centralize trades and functions; in a word, they want to squeeze out small industries, kill small business and thereby transform the majority of the bourgeoisie into wage-earners, and all this for the benefit of the so-called organizers, founders, directors, managers, advisers and shareholders of these gigantic concerns.

(1865)   *Pol. Cap.* p. 187

Just as the first duty of the Bank of France is to discount bills of exchange, so the first duty of the Land Bank is to help the tenant farmer to become the owner of his land.

(1863–64)   *Property* p. 41

[17] Cf. below, p. 166.

What we call tenant farming, which is a leftover from
the tyranny of the quiritary system,[18] hangs only by a
thread, namely the organization of a Bank that property
itself demands. It has been proved that land tends to return to those who cultivate it, and that leasing to tenant
farmers, like house rents and mortgage interest, is speculation of an abusive kind which reveals the disorder and ir-
regularities of the economic system . . . .

Once the land has been freed by the apparatus of revolution and agriculture liberated, feudal exploitation will
never be re-established. Let property then be sold, bought,
circulated, divided or accumulated, becoming completely
mobile; from the moment it is no longer shackled to the
ball and chain of ancient serfdom, it will have lost its intrinsic defects and will be completely transformed. It
will no longer be the same institution. However, let us
still call it by its old name, so dear to the heart of man
and so sweet to the peasant's ear: PROPERTY.

(1851)   *Revn.* pp. 260–61

Only products may be exchanged for products. Nobody
today disputes this maxim of political economy. Socialists
and economists alike accept it *de jure* and *de facto,* and
it provides a common ground on which opposing theories
may be reconciled and opinions meet to form one doctrine.

Exchange is either direct or indirect.

The chairmaker in Paris needs a cask of wine at the
same time as a Bordeaux wine merchant needs chairs.
The two producers can exchange their respective prod-

[18] *Ius quiritium* in Roman law denoted ownership based on
the body of rights of Roman citizenship. It was an aristocratic
concession to the plebs, giving them a limited form of land
ownership.

ucts by sending them to each other. This is direct exchange.

But let us suppose, as is usually the case, that one of the two people involved in the exchange does not need the other's product. For example, the Bordeaux wine merchant, instead of requiring chairs, requires calico; then exchange is no longer possible. The Parisian will pay for his wine with money, and the citizen of Bordeaux will use this money to have the material he requires sent from Mulhouse. This is indirect exchange.

Now this exchange, which is necessarily indirect because of the lack of any common credit link, would operate directly and without intermediaries were it possible for all those who wished to exchange goods in a country —all those who needed to buy and sell—to know one another. Let us imagine, for example, that the Parisian, the citizen of Mulhouse and the citizen of Bordeaux know at the same moment that each needs something: the first, a cask of wine, the second, chairs, and the third, a length of calico. It is clear that in this case the goods can be exchanged without any money having to be used. The Parisian will send his chairs to the manufacturer in Mulhouse, who will then send his calico to the producer in Bordeaux, and he in turn will send his wine to Paris. Substitute a hundred thousand people involved in exchanges for these three and it will still be the same, the exchange will still be direct.

What then must we do in order to allow direct exchange to take place—not simply between three, four, six, ten or a hundred people, but between a hundred thousand, or between all the producers and consumers in the world?

Something very simple. We must centralize all commercial transactions by means of one bank that will receive all the bills of exchange, money orders and promissory notes which represent the traders' invoices. Then we must generalize or convert these liabilities into vouchers that would be their equivalent and that consequently would be guaranteed by the products or real values that these liabilities represent.

Bank vouchers formed in this way would have all the qualities of the soundest bills.

They would not be subject to depreciation, since they would only be delivered against actual values and acceptable bills of exchange. Thus they would be based not on the products manufactured, but on those sold and delivered, and for which, consequently, repayment could be claimed.

There would be no problem of over-issuing since the voucher would only be delivered in exchange for bills of the first quality, that is to say, when there is a genuine and certain promise to repay.

Nobody would refuse to accept them since, as a result of the centralizing of all exchanges, and because all citizens would patronize the bank, they would represent for each person a value equal to the one that he would soon have to pay in bank vouchers.

(1848–49)   *Solution* pp. 182–84

The People's Bank[19]
DECLARATION

. . . . The People's Bank quite simply embodies the financial and economic aspects of the principle of modern democracy, that is, the sovereignty of the People, and of the republican motto, *Liberty, Equality, Fraternity.*

[19] Proudhon did try to found a system of free credit after the February Revolution of 1848. In January 1849 he officially registered the Act of Incorporation of what he called the People's Bank. It never managed to raise the capital of 50,000 francs, which Proudhon had decreed was necessary before it could function, and was wound up a few months after its foundation. Before the Bank had to close, it had reached a membership of 27,000, chiefly workers in associations or individual craftsmen.

I protest that when I criticized property, or more precisely the complex of institutions of which property is the foundation stone, I never meant to attack the rights of the individual as they were recognized by existing laws, nor to contest the legitimacy of acquired possessions, nor to cause goods to be shared out arbitrarily, nor to prevent property from being freely and regularly acquired through sale and exchange, nor to forbid or suppress, by sovereign decree, ground rent and interest on capital.

I believe that all these forms of human activity should remain free and optional for all. I allow no other modifications, restrictions or suppressions than those which are the natural, inevitable result of the universal application of the principle of reciprocity and of my proposed law of synthesis . . . .

ARTICLES OF THE COMPANY

Article 1. There is hereoy founded a commercial company under the name of the *People's Banking Company,* consisting of Citizen PROUDHON and all such persons as shall subscribe to these articles by becoming shareholders.

Article 2. The aim of the Company is to organize credit democratically . . . .

Article 9. The principles of the Company are as follows: That man is freely provided with raw materials by nature; That therefore in the economic order all products are the result of *labor* and all *capital* is unproductive; That as all *credit* transactions can be reduced to a form of *exchange,* capital loans and discounts cannot and must not bear interest.

Consequently, the People's Bank, which is to have as its *base* the essential gratuity of credit and exchange, as its *aim* the circulation of values not the production of them, and as its *means* the mutual consent of producers and consumers, can and must operate without capital.

Its aim will have been achieved when the whole body of producers and consumers have agreed to the Corporation's statutes.

Until this happens, the People's Banking Corporation, in conformity with established practice and the law, and in order to provide a stronger inducement to the public to subscribe, will build up its own capital . . . .

Article 16. The notes issued by the People's Bank shall be called *circulating vouchers* . . . .

Article 20. These circulating vouchers shall be accepted as legal tender by all subscribers to the Bank.

The Company shall not be bound to convert them into money. This is optional. But it shall guarantee that they will be accepted by all the subscribers. A complete list of their occupations, names and addresses shall at all times be displayed in the Company's offices.

Article 21. All subscribers shall undertake to obtain supplies, wherever possible, from other subscribers. They shall also undertake to supply only fellow subscribers.

Similarly, all producers and dealers who subscribe to the Bank shall undertake to supply their commercial and industrial products to their fellow subscribers at a reduced rate.

Article 22. Payment for transactions between the various subscribers to the People's Bank, that is to say for the reciprocal exchange of goods and services, shall be made by means of a note of the Bank, that is to say, a *circulating voucher* . . . .

Article 24. All subscribing and nonsubscribing consumers who wish to benefit from the reduced prices guaranteed by producers subscribing to the People's Bank will pay into it the sum of money they wish to spend, and will receive as cover an equal sum in circulating vouchers.

Article 25. The workers and wage-earners who wish to participate in the emancipating work of the People's Banking Company may, as it suits them, pay in the whole, or a part of their weekly wages. In exchange they will receive circulating vouchers.

Article 26. Traders, industrialists and producers of all kinds who would like to have the custom of the bearers of circulating vouchers and benefit from all the advantages provided by this new form of distribution may also become subscribers to the Company, thereby undertaking to accept the notes issued by the People's Bank as legal tender for all transactions.

Article 27. In order to facilitate the use of circulating vouchers, either the founder-members themselves, or subsidiary institutions with which they have agreements, or for which the Bank, as I will explain later, could provide credit, shall open bakeries, groceries and other essential industrial and commercial establishments in order to supply the requirements of those interested and to act as a channel for the circulating vouchers.

Article 28. The said establishments shall and must be independent of the Bank just as they must be independent of each other. They will be managed and run at the risk and sole responsibility of the entrepreneurs, and no one shall be accorded special privileges.

While it favors workers' associations, the People's Bank will uphold free trade and competition as the principle of all progress and guarantee of good quality and cheapness of goods . . . .

Article 30. No interest shall accrue on sums paid into the Bank in exchange for circulating vouchers . . . .

Article 41. The State for its loan certificates, manufacturers for their products, merchants for their merchandise, property owners, farmers and tenant farmers for their crops, holders of government bonds, in a word, all citizens may use the institution in order to obtain loans . . . .

Article 46. Although the People's Bank shall not give loans on mortgages, any more than it shall give loans against pledges, it shall give loans by opening credit accounts for property owners, whether traders or not, on long-term mortgage debentures and annuities.

Article 47. If the property owner has not paid back the loan within the required time, or if in two consecutive years he has not paid back the agreed annual installment, the Bank shall take steps to expropriate him.

Article 48. In cases where the Bank takes over the property, the principle shall be that preference shall be given to the expropriated person and his family for living on the property and running it in the capacity of tenant farmer or manager, upon conditions laid down by the Bank . . . .

Article 70. A committee composed of thirty representatives shall be set up to see to the management of the Bank and to represent the sleeping partners in their dealings with it.

They shall be chosen by the General Meeting from among the shareholders or subscribers in the various branches of production and public service.

Article 71. One third of the Committee of Inspection shall be re-elected each year. For the first two years the retiring members shall be chosen by ballot.

Any retiring member may be re-elected.

If a vacancy should occur during the year, a temporary replacement shall be provided by the Committee . . . .

Article 74. The General Meeting shall consist of not more than one thousand nominees of the general body of associates and subscribers.

Article 75. The representatives shall be elected according to industrial categories and in proportion to the number of subscribers and representatives there are in each category.

Before the elections the Bank's bulletin will publicize the number of representatives to be elected from each occupation and locality.

(1848–49)   *Solution* pp. 259–80

Citizens, you all know that citizen Proudhon has sought to set up an exchange organization to be for the people what the Bank of France is for the bankers. He at first called this the Exchange Bank, and then the People's Bank.

Our friend's aim was to rescue the working masses from capitalist exploitation. Consequently he had to try and reduce the interest on capital so that it represents simply the expenses which are necessary for running the People's Bank, that is to say, the wages of its employees plus the expenses covering the risks inherent in any operation of this kind. I would add in passing that the premiums for these risks will decrease proportionally according to the number of subscribers. When these conditions have been satisfied, credit will be free.

(1848–49)   *Solution* p. 285

V   EDUCATION

Let us therefore draw up a plan for educating the workers, without in any way prejudicing their literary instruction, which will be going on at the same time. It will allow the student to go through the whole range of industrial practices, working from the most simple to the most difficult without specializing in any one activity. The scheme will also bring out the principles underlying these practices, just as in the past the rudiments of science were deduced from the first industrial machines, and it will lead men mentally and physically toward the philosophy of labor which is the very triumph of liberty. By this method the industrial worker, the man of action and the intellectual will all be rolled into one. The result will be a person who is a scientist and philosopher to the tips of his fingers, who will be head and shoulders above the orthodox scientist and philosopher . . . .

When education in industry has been reformed according to the principles I have just elaborated, the workers' condition will be changed beyond recognition. The pain and repugnance that are now intimately associated with labor will gradually give way to a pleasure of heart and mind that will spring from labor itself. This is not to mention the profits from production, which will be all the more certain since there will be economic and social equilibrium . . . .

If social communion and solidarity among men are not merely empty words, let us imagine what the worker's education, his daily labor and his whole existence might be like. He would constantly be adding to and modifying the heritage left him by his fathers. They sowed the seed with enthusiasm; he will reap it with joy . . . .

Social communion and human solidarity is not a case of that passionate attraction which, according to Fourier, ought to flare up like fireworks in the setting of the *series of contrasting groups* from the intrigues of the *cabalist* tendency in man and the changes of his *butterfly* tendency.[20]

It is an inward pleasure, to be found as much in solitary meditative reflection as in the bustle of the workshop. It results from the worker's sense that he is making full use of his faculties—the strength of his body, the skill of his hands and the agility of his mind; it comes from his sense of pride at overcoming difficulties, at taming nature, at acquiring knowledge and at guaranteeing his independence. It is a sense of communion with the rest of the

[20] According to Charles Fourier, man is dominated by twelve principal passions: the five sensual passions, the four affective passions and the three active passions, including the *cabalist* (love of intrigue) and the *butterfly* (love of change) passions.

human race through the memory of past struggles, through identity of purpose and the equal sharing of well-being.

In these conditions, whatever the worker's link with what he is producing and whatever his relationship with his fellow workers, he enjoys the greatest privilege of which any man may boast, that of existing *of and by himself*. He has nothing in common with the beasts which consume without producing anything in return, *fruges consumere natae*.[21] He exploits everything given him by nature. And as he exploits nature he purifies it, makes it fertile and embellishes it. He restores to it more than he takes away. Even if he were to be taken away from the society of his fellows and carried off into the desert with his wife and children, he would discover within himself the seeds of all riches and would immediately set about founding a new human race.

If labor were developed and organized according to the principles of industrial growth and if it fulfilled all the required conditions of variety, health, intelligence, art, dignity, passion and legitimate gain (all of which it contains in essence), why should it not, even as far as pleasure is concerned, become preferable to games and dancing, fencing, gymnastics, entertainments and all the other distractions which man in his poverty has invented as a means of recovering from the mental and physical fatigue caused by being a slave to labor, by gentle exercise of mind and body? Would we not then have overcome the fatality of labor, just as we had previously overcome it in politics and economics?

WORKSHOP ORGANIZATION

But one might object that the savage, when he is not plagued by famine, illness, or war, spends his life, it is true, in a state of perpetual happiness. He is free, and within the limits of his intelligence he can call himself

21 "Formed by nature to consume the fruits of the earth."

king of creation. One can see why he instinctively wants to make no changes in his state. But the delight of civilized man each time he wrests a secret from nature or triumphs over inert matter by his labor is still greater. If we compare the advantages and disadvantages of primitive and civilized existence, we will find that the balance is undoubtedly in favor of the latter.

The idea of enabling the worker in a fully civilized state to enjoy the freedom of Eden and the benefits of labor, thanks to the simultaneous education of his mind and body, which give him access to the whole of acquired knowledge and thus secure his complete independence, certainly cannot be criticized. It is immensely far-reaching in its implications.

All the specialized branches of human activity are functions of each other. This means that all branches of industry make up one complete system. All the different, heterogeneous types of industry, which are not linked in any obvious way, and the countless numbers of trades and professions form one industry, one trade, one profession, one state.

Labor, like creation itself, is one and identical in plan, but infinitely varied in the forms it takes.

Therefore there is no reason why the apprenticeship of the workers should not be designed to embrace the whole of industrial activity instead of simply a fragment of it.

The consequences of such a system of education would be incalculable. Quite apart from economics, there would be a profound change in the human soul; the features of humanity would be completely altered. All traces of ancient degradation would disappear, transcendental vampirism would be eliminated, the spirit would be completely changed and civilization would move into a higher sphere. Labor would become divine, it would become the religion . . . .

The difficulties of carrying out such an educational plan stem from the division of labor. Most industries are built on this division and as a result seem to be ill-suited to deal with the variety of operations that are required. The division of labor appears to be all the more desirable since it does not demand knowledge from the workers, and this seems to be in keeping with man's natural inequality.

For in fact what use would general education be to the apprentice, if, once he had become a journeyman and chosen a trade, he were forced to spend the rest of his life in a humdrum mechanical job in some specialized branch of industry? Having been trained for glory, he would meet only martyrdom.

It must be noted that this objection does not hold good where the agricultural worker is concerned.

Agriculture, the hub of all industry, demands as much diversified knowledge as it demands diversified labor. It is destined to become the foremost of the arts and offers as much to the imagination as any artistic soul could wish for.

Furthermore, since it is usually a family affair, it gives the greatest possible guarantee of independence . . . .

Small industries do not present any problems either. They easily form associations with other industries or with agriculture. Far from being unwilling to accept this broad education, they consider it desirable since the worker can then easily change his job and circulate freely within the system of collective production as a coin circulates freely on the market.

We are therefore left with factories, mills, foundries, workshops and builders' yards, all the things which today we term *large-scale industry* and which are really industrial groups or combinations of separate types of employment. In these, manual skills have been replaced by perfected equipment and the roles of men and machines have been reversed. It is no longer the worker who uses his intelligence; this has been passed on to the machine. What ought to constitute the worker's pride has become a means of stultifying his mind. Spiritualism demonstrates in this way that soul and body are separate and can proudly boast that it has produced its masterpiece . . . .

All workers ought to receive full instruction both about each specialized industry and about the whole field of industry. Thus all large-scale industrial establishments where there is a division of functions can serve as workshop and school, both theoretical and practical, for workers who are serving an apprenticeship or who are not yet associates.

It is the duty of all citizens who are destined for industry during the time they are apprentices or journeymen to pay their debts to labor, and this quite apart from the public services they must also perform. This they will do for a fixed time and for an appropriate wage, by working in all sections of the establishment in turn. Later they will, as associates or masters, be entitled to participate in the management and share in the profits.

Having benefited from the ability he has acquired during his first apprenticeship, it is very much in the young worker's interest to increase his knowledge and improve his aptitudes by further study in other branches of industry. This he is encouraged to do until such time as he can with honor and advantage finally settle down in one occupation.

In short, polytechnical education and the possibility of rising through all the grades guarantees the worker's emancipation. *Apprentice,* JOURNEYMAN, MASTER, this is what we may all expect from the future.

(1858) *Justice* III, pp. 86–93

Where do you expect the State to obtain sums of this kind [400, 800, 1200 million francs a year]? The simplest calculation proves that in society's present state, educating the young, with the exception of a privileged élite, is a philanthropic dream; like poverty, ignorance is inherent in the condition of the worker, and the intellectual inferiority of the working classes cannot be overcome. In a political system based on hierarchy with a capitalist and industrial feudalism, and having an anarchical commercial system, such education, although in itself desirable, would be totally wasteful and, moreover, dangerous. It has not been without good reason that statesmen of all ages, although they may have been concerned with educating the people, have reduced this education to very simple forms. They have all seen that at a higher level it would become disruptive, and that by overloading people's faculties it would constitute a grave danger to society and even to labor itself . . . .

Well, things that are totally and radically impossible under the present system can easily be accomplished under a mutualist system. This will simply do what has always been done but in a more co-ordinated fashion and more intelligently, with a true feeling for the rights of the masses, though with no thought of innovating.

Here, summed up in a few words, is the system.

1. All heads of families ought to be in a position to defray the initial costs of their children's education from the time of their birth to the age of seven or eight, through the exchange of goods or services. This will be made possible for the father of the family by economic reform, which is not the question we are dealing with at the moment.

2. From the age of seven to eighteen, the education and instruction of the young will be continued either at home by the parents themselves, if they wish it, or in private schools they will set up and direct at their own expense, if they prefer not to entrust their children to the State schools. Parents and communes will be allowed the greatest possible freedom in this matter. The State will only intervene to aid in areas which are beyond the scope of parents or communes.

3. State schools will be run on the principle that pro-

fessional training must be combined with scientific and literary studies. Consequently children from the age of nine and perhaps less will be obliged to do some useful, productive manual work; the expenses of their education will be more than covered by what the pupils produce.

This is already the case in peasant families, where the children are employed from an early age at work in the fields while they are being taught in the village schools. This is also true in trade and industry where the apprentices, who are sometimes paid wages and sometimes not, pay for their apprenticeship with their labor while at the same time they continue to study mathematics, drawing, etc. . . . .

Workers' associations have a very important role to play here. Linked to the system of public education, they will become both centers of production and centers for education. Fathers will continue to supervise their children. The working masses will be in daily contact with the youthful army of agricultural and industrial workers. Labor and study, which have for so long and so foolishly been kept apart, will finally emerge side by side in their natural state of union. Instead of being confined to narrow, specialized fields, vocational education will include a variety of different types of work which, taken as a whole, will insure that each student becomes an all-round worker. Free enterprise will gain by this, and the security of family and State will benefit from it to an even greater extent. The contract of apprenticeship placed under the protection of public education, will, by the power of this great new institution, be converted into a mutualist agreement between all the fathers of families in the different trades and professions who will, in a manner of speaking, simply be exchanging children . . . .

I maintain that within a system of industrial association, political federation and mutualist guarantees, nothing could be easier than organizing a system of education and teaching that should include both scientific and vocational training, board and lodging—all for the equivalent of no more than sixteen hundred million a year. In fact it would cost the family, the commune or the State NOTHING AT ALL.

(1865)   *Pol. Cap.* pp. 341–43

VI   ANARCHY

What form of government will we consider best? "How can you ask?" one of my youngest readers might reply, "You are a republican." Republican, yes, but this word has no precise meaning. *Res publica*, that is, the public good. Now whoever desires the public good, under whatever form of government, can call himself a republican. Kings too are republicans. "Well then, are you a democrat?" No. "What, you cannot be a monarchist!" No. "A Constitutionalist?" Heaven forbid! "Then you must be for the aristocracy." Not at all. "Do you want a mixed government?" Even less. "What are you then?" I am an anarchist.

"I understand, you are being satirical at the expense of government." Not in the least. I have just given you my considered and serious profession of faith. Although I am a strong supporter of order, I am in the fullest sense of the term, an anarchist.

(1840)   *Memoir,* p. 335

In any given society, the authority man has over man is in inverse ratio to the intellectual level of development reached by that society. The probable duration of that authority may be calculated according to the more or less widespread desire for true government, that is, government based on science. Just as the right of force and

the right of artfulness are limited by the ever-increasing
bounds of justice, and will finally be eclipsed by equality,
so the sovereignty of will is giving way to the sovereignty
of reason, and must finally vanish within a form of scientific socialism. Property and royalty have been decaying
since the world began. Just as man seeks justice in equality, society seeks order in anarchy.

Anarchy, that is the absence of a ruler or a sovereign.[22]
This is the form of government we are moving closer to
every day. Because of the deep-rooted habit of taking one
man as representing order and of taking his will as law,
people regard us as the very summit of disorder and the
embodiment of chaos. There is a story about a Parisian
bourgeois in the seventeenth century who heard that in
Venice they did not have a king. The fellow could not get
over his amazement and thought he would die of laughter
when he first heard of such a ridiculous thing. We all
share this prejudice. Every one of us wants a leader or
leaders. I have in my possession at this moment a pamphlet
written by an ardent communist who is dreaming, like a
second Marat, of dictatorship. The most advanced among
us are those who want the greatest possible number of
sovereigns. Their most ardent wish is for the royal power
to be enshrined in the National Guard. Doubtless some
person who is jealous of the citizens' militia will soon
say, "Every man is king." But my reply to this will be,
"No man is king. We are all, whether we like it or not,
partners." All questions of domestic policy must be settled
in the light of Departmental[23] statistics. All questions
of foreign policy are a matter of international statistics.
The science of government belongs by right to one of the
branches of the Academy of Science, whose permanent

[22] The meaning usually given to the word *anarchy* is absence
of principles, absence of laws. This is how it has become
synonymous with *disorder*. (Proudhon's footnote)

[23] The Department is the main unit of local administration
in France.

secretary must necessarily become Prime Minister. Since citizens may lay a memorandum before the Academy, all citizens are lawmakers. But since no person's opinion carries any weight unless it is supported by facts, no one person's will can override reason, and therefore no one is king . . . .

What then are the people if they are not sovereign and if they are not the source of legislative power? The people are the guardians of the law. The people constitute the *executive power*. Any citizen may affirm that such and such a thing is true or just, but his conviction binds no one other than himself. If the truth which he is proclaiming is to become law, then it must be generally recognized as such. But what is recognizing a law? It is verifying a mathematical or metaphysical calculation. It is repeating an experiment, observing a phenomenon or taking note of a fact. Only the whole nation has a right to say "Mandons et ordonnons."[24]

(1840)   *Memoir* pp. 339–40

I wrote in 1840 the following profession of my political faith, remarkable for both its laconism and its vigor: *I am an anarchist,* declaring by this word the negation—or better—the insufficiency, of the principle of authority. That is to say, as I later showed, that the notion of authority, like the notion of an absolute being, is only an analytic concept that is powerless to provide a constitution for society, regardless of the source of authority and the manner in which it is exercised. For authority and politics I substituted the notion of ECONOMICS—a positive, synthetic idea which, as I see it, is alone capable of leading to a rational, practical conception of social order. Moreover, in this I was simply taking up Saint Simon's thesis,

[24] "We command and we ordain": the executive formula of the French kings.

which has been so strangely distorted by his disciples, and is disputed today by M. Enfantin[25] for tactical reasons that I cannot fathom. This thesis consists of saying, in the light of history and of the incompatibility of the notions of authority and progress, that society is in the process of completing the governmental cycle for the last time; that the public reason has become convinced that politics is powerless to improve the lot of the masses; that the notions of power and authority are being replaced in people's minds, as in the course of history, by the notions of labor and exchange; and that the end result is the substitution of economic organizations for political machinery, etc., etc.

(1853) *Progress* p. 74

I have already mentioned ANARCHY, or the government of each man by himself—or as the English say, *self-government*—as being one example of the liberal regime. Since the expression "anarchical government" is a contradiction in terms, the system itself seems to be impossible and the idea absurd. However, it is only language that needs to be criticized. The notion of *anarchy* in politics is just as rational and positive as any other. It means that once industrial functions have taken over from political functions, then business transactions and exchange alone produce the social order. In these conditions each man could call himself his own master, which is the very opposite of constitutional monarchy.

(1863) *Fed.* p. 278

By the word [Anarchy] I wanted to indicate the extreme limit of political progress. *Anarchy* is, if I may be

[25] Prosper Enfantin had led the Saint-Simonians after their "Master's" death in the founding of a hierarchic Church.

permitted to put it this way, a form of government or constitution in which public and private consciousness, formed through the development of science and law, is alone sufficient to maintain order and guarantee all liberties. In it, as a consequence, the institutions of the police, preventive and repressive methods, officialdom, taxation, etc., are reduced to a minimum. In it, more especially, the forms of monarchy and intensive centralization disappear, to be replaced by federal institutions and a pattern of life based on the commune. When politics and home life have become one and the same thing, when economic problems have been solved in such a way that individual and collective interests are identical, then—all constraint having disappeared—it is evident that we will be in a state of total liberty or anarchy. Society's laws will operate by themselves through universal spontaneity, and they will not have to be ordered or controlled.

When you come to the articles on *God and Property*,[26] do please let me know. You will see from my few words of explanation that the propositions, *God is evil* and *Property is theft,* are not mere paradoxes. Although I maintain their literal meaning, I no more want to make it a crime to believe in God than I do to abolish Property.

(August 20, 1864)   *C* 14, p. 32

To Mr. X***

The community seeks *equality* and *law*. Property, which is born of the autonomy of reason and respect for individual merit, wants above all things *independence* and *proportionality*.

But the community, mistaking uniformity for law, and leveling down for equality, becomes tyrannical and unjust. Property, through its despotism and its infringement

---

[26] In the dictionary being compiled by the recipient of this letter.

of rights, soon becomes oppressive and works against the interests of society.

What the community and property intend is good, but what they both in fact produce is bad. Why should this be so? It is because each is exclusive and each overlooks two elements in society. The community rejects independence and proportionality, while property does not fulfill the conditions of equality and law.

Now if we imagine a society based on these four principles—equality, law, independence and proportionality, we will find that:

1. Since equality means only *equality of conditions,* that is, of *means,* not *equality of well-being*—this, when the means are equal, must be the worker's responsibility —equality is in no sense a violation of justice and equity.

2. *Law,* being based on the science of observed facts and consequently on necessity itself, is in no way detrimental to independence.

3. The personal *independence* of individuals or the autonomy of private judgment, which is the result of differences of talent and ability, does not constitute a danger, provided it remains within the limits of the law.

4. Proportionality, since it is only tolerated in the realm of thought and feeling and not in physical things, may be observed without violating justice or social equality.

I will term this third form of society, which is a synthesis of the community and of property, LIBERTY.

(1840)   *Memoir* p. 342

In my attacks on property from 1840 onward, I was careful to protest in the name of liberty against State control as well as against communism. I have always had a particular horror of regimentation; from the first, when I declared myself an anarchist, I loathed centralized, monarchical absolutism. In 1848 I declared my opposition to the State control advocated in the report of the Luxembourg Commission. I praised the Provisional Government for the caution it showed in dealing with social reform, and since then I have declared many times that their restraint, so often criticized, was in my view entirely praiseworthy. My hostility toward the principle of authority has in no way diminished. The studies of history I have been pursuing in my spare time for the last ten years have convinced me that it is the curse of society. Apart from a handful of bigots, the workers were not communist in France in 1848, nor in '89, '93 or '96. The failure of their communist experiments reduced the first utopians to despair . . . . and in France it is only a misconception of the notion of equality.

Liberty is man's right to make use of his faculties, and to do so as he pleases. But there can be no doubt that it does not include the right to abuse. We must, however, make a distinction between two types of abuse. In the first case it is the *abuser* alone who suffers the consequences; in the second, another person's rights are infringed, i.e. his right to liberty and his right to make free use of land or materials. So long as only the person affected is the one who is guilty of the abuse, society has no right to intervene; should it do so, it is itself guilty of an abuse. In this case the citizen must be governed only by his reason. He would be unworthy and lacking in self-respect if he were to accept any rule other than that of his own free will. I will go further and add that society must be organized in such a way as to make abuses of this second kind increasingly impossible, so that there will be less and less need to intervene to suppress them. If it is not—if society moves closer and closer toward communism instead of toward anarchy or the government of man by himself (in English: *self-government*)—then the social organization itself will be an abuse of man's faculties.

(1863–64)   Property pp. 28–29

Instead of sharing the absolutist view that government is the organ and expression of society, or the doctrinaire view that it is an instrument for order, or rather for policing, or the radical view that it is a means for revolution, let us try to see it simply as a phenomenon of social existence, the external embodiment of our rights, the educating of one of our faculties. Who knows, we might discover that the various forms of government over which nations and citizens have been cutting each other's throats for sixty centuries are nothing more than a phantasmagoria in our minds, and that the first duty of freely exercised reason is to relegate them to the museum and the library . . . .

What the citizen seeks in a government, whether he calls it King, Emperor or President, is himself, and it is LIBERTY.

Apart from Humanity there is no God; the concept of theology is meaningless. Apart from Liberty there is no Government; the concept of politics is valueless.

The best form of government, like the most perfect religion, taken literally is a contradictory idea. The problem is to discover how we can obtain not the best government but the greatest freedom. The only reality of power and politics is a liberty equal to and identical with order. How is this absolute liberty, which is synonymous with order, constituted? We will learn the answer from the analysis of the various forms that authority takes. As for the rest, we no more accept the government of man by man than we accept the exploitation of man by man . . . .

Like industrial liberty, political liberty will for us be the result of mutual guarantees. It is through guaranteeing each other's liberty that we will be able to do without this government whose objective it is to exemplify the republican motto: *Liberty, Equality, Fraternity*, leaving to our intelligence the task of bringing it about.

(1849)   *Confessions* pp. 61–62, 64

What is the *Social Contract?* Is it an agreement between citizen and government? No, for this would still be to remain trapped within the same idea. The social contract is an agreement between man and man, from which what we call society must emerge. Here the notion of *commutative justice,* established by the primitive fact of exchange and defined by Roman law, is replaced by that of *distributive justice,* which has been dismissed without appeal by the Republican critics. Translate the legal terms *contract* and *commutative justice* into the language of affairs, and you have COMMERCE. That is, in its most elevated sense, the action by which men, declaring themselves to be essentially producers, renounce all claims to governing each other.

Commutative justice, rule by contract, or in other words, *rule by economics and industry,* those are all different synonyms expressing the idea whose advent must abolish the old systems of *distributive justice, rule by laws,* or to be more concrete, the feudal, governmental or military regime. The future of mankind lies in this change . . . .

The notion of contract precludes that of government. M. Ledru-Rollin,[27] who is a jurist and whose attention I would draw to this fact, must already be aware of it. The contract, or commutative agreement, is characterized by the fact that it increases man's liberty and well-being. The

[27] One of the leaders of the Jacobin Republicans, who stood as the Republican presidential candidate in the elections of December 1848, which Louis Napoleon won. Proudhon had supported the socialist-republican nominee, Raspail. Ledru-Rollin represented for Proudhon the Jacobin tradition of political action in contrast to his own emphasis on the primacy of economic and social forces.

setting up of any authority, on the other hand, necessarily decreases it. This is evident if one reflects that a contract is an act by which two or more individuals agree to organize among themselves, within certain limits and for a given time, the industrial force which we call exchange. Consequently they undertake mutual obligations and make reciprocal guarantees for a certain number of services, products, benefits, duties and so on which they are in a position to obtain and render, knowing themselves to be in all other respects totally independent, both in what they consume and what they produce.

Between the contracting parties there is necessarily a real and personal interest involved. The word contract implies that a man negotiates with the intention of securing his liberty and his income at the same time, without there being any possibility of compensation. Between governing and governed, on the contrary—whatever the system of representation or delegation of the governmental power—some part of the citizen's liberty and fortune is necessarily alienated. What advantages does he gain in their place? This we have already explained.

A contract is therefore essentially bilateral. It imposes no obligations on the contracting parties other than those resulting from their personal promise of reciprocal service. It is subject to no outside authority. It is the only law that binds the parties. It expects to be fulfilled at their instigation alone.

If such is "contract" in its widest sense and as it is applied from day to day, how can we describe the Social Contract which is supposed to unite all the members of a State in a common interest?

The Social Contract is the supreme act by which each citizen pledges to society his love, his intelligence, his labor, his services, his products and his goods in exchange for the affection, ideas, works, products, services and goods of his fellow citizens. What each man may claim is always determined by what he contributes; as he makes his contributions, so will he receive his compensation.

Thus the social contract must include the whole body of citizens, their interests and relations. If even one man were excluded from the contract, if even one problem which the citizens, who are intelligent, industrious and sensitive, were called upon to deal with were omitted, the contract would be more or less partial and exclusive. It could not be called social . . . .

Furthermore, the social contract being discussed here is in no way similar to the contract with society. By the latter . . . . the contracting party alienates some of his liberty and submits to a solidarity of a burdensome and often hazardous kind in the somewhat dubiously grounded hope of gain. The social contract is of the nature of the commutative contract. Not only does it leave the contracting party free, but it also increases his freedom. Not only does it leave him all his possessions, but it also actually increases his property. It makes no stipulations with regard to his labor; it is concerned only with exchange. None of those things is true of the contract with society; in fact, they are all completely contrary to it.

(1851)   Revn. pp. 187–89

The notion of Government is succeeded by that of Contract. The course of history inevitably leads mankind to adopt new practices. Economic criticism has already noted that under the new system political institutions must disappear within industrial organization. Let us therefore fearlessly conclude that the revolutionary slogan can no longer be *Direct Legislation, Direct Government, Simplified Government*. It must be NO MORE GOVERNMENT.

There must be no monarchy, no aristocracy, no democracy even, insofar as this implies a government acting in the name of the people and claiming to be the people. No authority, no government, even if it be popular government; this is the Revolution.

(1851)   *Revn.* p. 199

We have already explained that we would substitute industrial organization for government.

Instead of laws we would have contracts. No laws would be passed, either by majority vote or unanimously. Each citizen, each commune or corporation, would make its own laws.

Instead of political power we would have economic forces.

Instead of the old class divisions between citizen, noble and commoner, bourgeoisie and proletariat, we would have categories and classes relating to various functions: agriculture, industry, commerce and so on.

Instead of public forces we would have collective forces.

Instead of standing armies we would have industrial companies.

Instead of a police force, we would have a collective interest.

Instead of political centralization we would have economic centralization.

What need have we of government when a state of harmony has been reached? Surely the National Bank with all its branches provides us with centralization and unity? Surely the agreements made between farm laborers for the compensation, liquidation and redemption of agrarian estates create unity? Do not the workers' companies formed for the development of the large industries also create unity in a different way? And is not also the constitution of value, the contract of contracts as we have called it, the highest and most indestructible form of unity?

If I have to convince you by providing examples of precedents within your own experience: has not the system of weights and measures, the greatest monument to the Convention,[28] formed for the last fifty years the cornerstone of economic unity, which through the progress of ideas is destined to replace political unity?

Therefore ask no further questions as to what we would have instead of government, nor what will become of society when there are no longer governments. I warrant that in future it will be easier to conceive of society without a government than it will be to conceive of society with one.

(1851)   Revn. pp. 302–3

The Revolution has not in fact suppressed the occult, mystic power which used to be called the sovereign, but which we prefer to call the State. It has not reduced society simply to a collection of individuals who come to terms and make contracts with each other and through their free transactions bind themselves by a common law, as Rousseau's *Social Contract* led us to believe. No, the notion of Government, Power or State, whatever one may like to call it, has remained intact beneath the ruins of the *ancien régime* and is stronger than ever before. One thing that the Revolution has altered is the place accorded to Liberty, its new civil and political status.

Let us note, moreover, that the State as conceived by the Revolution is not something purely abstract, a sort of legal fiction, as Rousseau and others have supposed. It is as positive a reality as society itself and as the individual himself. The State is the collective power that results from any grouping together of men, from their mutual relations, from the identity of their interests, from their communal actions and from the force of their opinions and passions. The State does not of course exist without the citizens. Its existence is neither prior to nor superior to

[28] Of 1792–95.

theirs. It exists rather by virtue of the fact that they exist, distinct from each individual, and from the whole, on account of its special faculties and attributes. Nor is liberty a fictitious power consisting simply of the faculty of choosing between action and inaction. It is a positive faculty, *sui generis*, which is to the individual, who is a collection of different passions and faculties, what the State is to the collective body of citizens—namely, the greatest power of man's design and development.

This is why reasons of State[29] and individual reasons are not the same thing, why interests of State are not the same as private interests, even if these were to be identical for the majority or even the whole body of citizens, and why the acts of the government are different than the acts of the private individual. Just as there is a difference between the individual and the community, so there is a difference between the faculties, attributes and interests of the citizen and those of the State. We have a good example of this in the principle I put forward that the laws of exchange are not the same for the individual as they are for the State.

Under the system based on Divine Right, reason of State was bound up with dynastic, aristocratic or clerical reason, and thus it did not always accord with the principle of justice. This is why modern law has proscribed the unsound principle of "reason of State." Similarly, the interests of the State were bound up with the interests of the dynasty or class, and thus these too were not always in accordance with Justice. This is why all societies that have been transformed by Revolution tend toward a republican government.

Under the new regime, on the contrary, reason of State must in all things conform to the spirit of Justice, which truly expresses what is right. These reasons are essentially general and synthetic, and consequently differ from the

[29] *Raison d'État,* here and throughout this passage.

reasons of the citizen, which are always more or less specific and individual. Similarly, the interests of the State have been purged of all aristocratic and dynastic claims. The interests of the State are, above all, higher interests of law and this implies that they are different in nature from private interests.

The author of the *Social Contract* may well claim, and his followers may well repeat, that the true sovereign is the citizen, that the king, who is an organ of the State, is merely the people's delegate, and consequently that the State belongs to the citizens. It may have been right to say this at a time when the rights of man and of the citizen needed to be claimed, and when liberty had to be ushered in in the place of despotism. But at present the Revolution encounters no more obstruction, at least none from the *ancien régime*. What we must do is fully understand its ideas and put them into practice. In this context Rousseau's language is no longer correct; I would even go so far as to call it false and dangerous.

(1861) *Taxation* pp. 64–66

VII FEDERALISM

All political conditions and all forms of government, including federalism, may be reduced to the following formula: *the balancing of authority by liberty,* and vice versa. It is as a consequence of this that the categories *monarchy, aristocracy, democracy, etc.,* used since Aristotle by so many writers to classify governments, to distinguish between forms of states and to make distinctions between nations, can all, except for federalism, be shown to be hypothetical constructions based on mere experience, which are barely able to satisfy the demands of reason and justice . . . .

Two different forms of government may be deduced *a priori* from these two fundamental notions [authority and liberty], according to which one is given preference, namely, *Government based on Authority* and *Government based on Liberty.*

Furthermore, since society is composed of individuals, and since the relation of the individual to the group may be thought of in four different ways so far as politics is concerned, there are as a result four forms of governments, two for each system.

1. *Government based on Authority*

A. The government of all men by one man, that is, MONARCHY OR PATRIARCHY.

a. Government of all men by all men, that is PANARCHY or COMMUNISM.[30]

The essential feature of this system, in both its forms, is that there is no division of power.

2. *Government based on Liberty*

B. The government of all men by each man, that is DEMOCRACY.

b. The government of each man by himself, that is *anarchy* or *self-government.*

The essential feature of this system, in both its forms, is the division of power.

(1863)   *Fed.* pp. 272–74

Since the two principles, Authority and Liberty, which underlie all forms of organized society, are on the one

---

[30] Proudhon says later, *Fed.* p. 276, about communism: "this political system is rare; indeed there may well be no examples of it at all. Authority weighs more heavily and the individual is oppressed to a greater extent than in any other system. It has seldom been adopted except by religious associations, which in all countries and in all creeds have tended to destroy liberty."

hand contrary to each other, in a perpetual state of conflict, and on the other can neither eliminate each other nor be resolved, some kind of compromise between the two is necessary. Whatever the system favored, whether it be monarchical, democratic, communist or anarchist, its length of life will depend on the extent to which it has taken the contrary principle into account.

For example . . . . in a democratic government it is no good trying, however wisely or judiciously, to determine the rights and obligations of citizens, the functions of officials or trying to foresee everything that might arise, all possible exceptions and anomalies: the fecundity of the unexpected far outstrips any foresight on the part of the statesman, and more legislation only gives rise to more litigation. This requires of those in power both initiative and powers of arbitration, which can only succeed if they are based on authority. Deprive Democracy and Liberty of the supreme sanction of Authority, and the State will immediately collapse. It is clear, however, that if this is so we are no longer operating in the sphere of freedom of contract, unless one maintains that in cases of litigation the citizens have specifically agreed to abide by the decision of one of their number, namely a magistrate nominated in advance. But to do this latter means rejecting the principle of democracy in favor of acting like a monarchy.

However much democracy increases the number of legal guarantees and methods of control as its number of civil servants grows, however much it surrounds its administrators by formalities, and however frequently it calls upon citizens to vote, its civil servants will still be men vested with authority, as the saying goes. And if one or more public servants were to be responsible for the overall control of affairs, this head of government, whether an individual or a group, would be in effect what Rousseau himself called a *prince*, only just short of being a king.

Similar observations may be made about communism and anarchy. There has never been an example of a perfect community, and it is unlikely, whatever degree of civilization, morality and wisdom man may reach, that all trace of government and authority will disappear. But while the community is the dream of most socialists, anarchy is the ideal of the economists' school of thought, which boldly aims at abolishing all forms of government and constituting society solely on the basis of property and free labor.

I will not give any further examples. What I have just said is sufficient to demonstrate the truth of my proposition, namely, that Monarchy, Democracy, Communism and Anarchy are all unable to realize their ideals on their own, and thus they are reduced to complementing each other by means of mutual borrowings.

(1863)   *Fed.* pp. 288, 290–91

Since government based on liberty and contract is daily gaining ground over government based on authority, we must focus our attention on the notion of contract, for this is the dominant idea in politics . . . .

The political contract only attains full dignity and morality on condition that it is firstly synallagmatic and commutative,[31] and secondly that its aims are kept within certain limits—two conditions which are supposed to be part of the democratic system, but which are more often than not a fiction. In a representative and centralized

[31] Proudhon, *Fed.* pp. 315–16, defines these terms by quoting articles 1102 and 1104 of the Napoleonic Civil Code of 1804: "A contract is *synallagmatic* or bilateral when the contracting parties bind themselves by mutual obligations." "A contract is *commutative* when each of the parties undertakes to give or to do something which is considered as the equivalent of what is given or done for him. When the equality consists of the chance of gain or loss in circumstances of uncertainty, the contract is called *aleatory*."

democracy, in a constitutional monarchy based on a property qualification, or more particularly in a communist republic like Plato's, can one say that the contract which binds the citizen to the State is equal and reciprocal? Can one say that a contract which deprives the citizen of half or a third of his sovereignty and a quarter of his product, is kept within just limits? As experience all too often confirms, it would be truer to say that the contract in all these systems is grossly unfair and *onerous* since it largely makes no compensations. It is also largely *aleatory* since the promised advantages, which in any case are insufficient, are not even guaranteed.

If the political contract is to fulfill the condition of being synallagmatic and commutative, as the idea of democracy suggests, and if it is to be kept within reasonable limits and be advantageous and useful to everyone, then firstly the citizen must, when he makes the contract, receive from the State as much as he himself gives. Secondly, he must retain his freedom, sovereignty and initiative, except where these are needed for the particular object that is the purpose of the contract and that the State is being requested to guarantee. If it is regulated and interpreted in this way, the political contract is what I would term a *federation*.

FEDERATION, from the Latin *fœdus*, gen. *fœderis*, that is to say pact, contract, treaty, convention, alliance, etc., is an agreement by which one or several heads of a family, one or several communes, one or several groups of communes or states, bind themselves by mutual and equal agreements for one or several determinate aims, for which the responsibility falls specifically and exclusively on the members of the federation.[32]

[32] In Rousseau's theory, adopted by Robespierre and the Jacobins, the social contract is a legal fiction invented to account for the formation of the State and for the relationship between government and the individual, to avoid appealing to divine law, paternal authority or social necessity. This the-

To return to this definition.

The essence and nature of the federal contract is that in this system the contracting parties, heads of families, cantons, provinces or States not only bind themselves synallagmatically and commutatively, but that in making the agreement they assure themselves individually more rights, liberty, authority and property than they give up . . . .

Any agreement, even a synallagmatic and commutative one, that demands the associates' total effort deprives them of their independence and forces them to devote themselves solely to the association; it is excessive and hateful to both citizens and men.

(1863)   *Fed.* pp. 315, 317–19

To sum up, the federal system is the very reverse of hierarchy or centralized administration and government. Hierarchy is the distinguishing feature common, *ex aequo*,[33] to imperial democracy, constitutional monarchy and republics. The basic distinguishing law of a federation is that, as more states join the Confederation, the powers of the central authority become increasingly specialized and restricted in number, range and, so to speak, intensity. On the other hand in a centralized government, in proportion to any increase in land or population, the power of the supreme authority increases, reaches further, and becomes more direct—bringing the affairs of

---

ory, which was borrowed from the Calvinists, in 1764 marked a step forward since it provided a rational explanation for what had previously been considered as belonging to natural law and religion. In the federal system the social contract is more than a fiction. It is a positive, effective pact that is actually proposed, discussed, voted on and adopted, and which can be modified at will by the contracting parties. The federal contract is as far from Rousseau's and that of '93 as reality is from the hypothetical. (Proudhon's footnote)

[33] "To an equal degree."

provinces, communes, corporations and private individuals under the direct control of the prince. The result of this is that liberty, not only at the communal and provincial level, but also at the individual and national level, is completely suppressed.

(1863)   *Fed.* p. 321

In a free society the role of the State or Government is essentially one of legislating, initiating, creating, inaugurating and setting up; it should be as little as possible one of executing. In this respect the term *executive power,* which describes one of the features of sovereign power, has been very misleading. The State does not undertake public works, for this would identify it with industrialists who undertake public contracts. Whether it decrees, acts or oversees, the State is the instigator and supreme guide of all developments. If it sometimes takes a hand in the work itself, it is in order to set things in motion and give an example. Once a new service has been created, once it has been installed and set up, the State withdraws and leaves the local authority and citizens in charge of operating it.

The State is responsible for deciding weights and measures, and it decides the standard, value and units of currency. When the models have been provided and the first issue completed, the minting of gold, silver and copper coins ceases to be a public responsibility. It is no longer in the hands of the State or its Ministries, but must be left in the hands of the towns and nothing should prevent it from being entirely free, in the same way as the making of scales, weighing machines, barrels and bottles. The only law that should operate here is that of maintaining the lowest possible price. What are the standards operating in France to decide whether gold and silver coins may be accepted as standard? They are that the coins should be composed of one tenth alloy and nine tenths fine metal.

I am all in favor of inspection and control during the minting, but the role of the State should go no further than this.

My remarks about money are also true of countless services which are wrongly left in government hands, namely, roads, canals, tobacco, the postal and telegraph service, the railways and so on. I quite understand, accept, and if need be demand the principle of State intervention in these large-scale public services. What I do not see is why they should still be subject to State control once they have been handed over to the public. Centralization of this kind seems to me to indicate excessive power. In 1848 I asked the State to set up national banks, credit institutions, provident funds and insurance organizations, as well as railways. It never occurred to me that the State should from then on be a banker, insurance agent, carrier and so on when once its initial functions had been completed. I do not of course think that the education of the people can be organized without considerable help from the State, but I nevertheless believe firmly in the freedom of education, as I do in the freedom of everything else. I want education to be as separate from the State as is the Church itself . . . .

Is it really necessary that the courts should be dependent on the central authority? I know that it has always been the highest prerogative of the prince to dispense justice. But this prerogative is a relic of the time of divine right and cannot be claimed by a constitutional monarch, let alone by the head of an Empire based on universal suffrage. Once the idea of Law has again become manmade and gained thereby predominance in the political system, then the independence of the magistrature will necessarily follow. To consider Justice as an attribute of the central or federal authority is repugnant, for Justice can never be delegated other than to the municipal or, at the most, to the provincial authority. Justice is the essential characteristic of man, which should never be surrendered up for any reasons of national interest. I do not even allow military affairs to be an exception to this rule. The militia, the munition depots, the fortresses, should only pass into the hands of the federal authorities in the actual event of war and for the particular purpose of that war. Otherwise soldiers and munitions should remain in the hands of the local authorities.

In a well-regulated society everything must be in a continual state of growth; science, industry, labor, wealth, public health, liberty and morality must move forward at the same pace. Activity and life must not be suspended for an instant. The State, which is the principal moving force, is always active, for there are always new demands to be satisfied and new problems to be solved. While its functions as prime mover and overall director never come to an end, this does not imply that it ever repeats itself in what it produces. This is the ultimate expression of progress. Now what happens when—and we see examples of this everywhere and all the time—it retains control of the services it has created and succumbs to the temptation of monopolizing? It changes from being a founder to being a worker. It is no longer the fertile, enriching, guiding spirit of the community, which at the same time imposes no restraint, but is rather a vast limited liability company with six hundred thousand employees and six hundred thousand soldiers entirely at its disposal. Instead of serving citizens and communes, it disinherits and exploits them, and it is not long before corruption, dishonesty and slackness creep into the system. The State is so engrossed in maintaining its position, increasing its prerogatives and services and enlarging its budget, that it loses sight of its true function and degenerates into autocracy and conservatism. Society suffers, and, going against historical law, the nation starts to decay.

(1863)   *Fed.* pp. 326–29

Once the federal government has reformed the political system it will then necessarily undertake a series of economic reforms. Here is a brief indication of the nature of these reforms.

Just as for political reasons two or more independent States may form a federation in order to guarantee their frontiers or to protect their liberties, so for economic reasons federations may be formed to insure the protection of commerce and industry. This latter is called a *customs union*. Other kinds of federations may be formed for the construction and maintenance of systems of communication such as roads, canals and railways, or for the organization of credit and insurance, etc. The aim of these private federations is to protect the citizens of the member States from being exploited by capitalists and bankers either at home or abroad. Their union, in opposition to the financial feudalism[34] predominant today, forms what I would call an *agrarian-industrial federation*.

(1863)   *Fed.* p. 357

When it is translated into the realm of politics, what we have hitherto termed mutualism or guaranteeism is called *federalism*. The entire political and economic revolution is summed up in this simple synonym.

(1865)   *Pol. Cap.* p. 198

Europe would be too large to form a single confederation; it would have to be a confederation of confederations. This is why I pointed out in my most recent publication[35]

---

[34] Cf. below, p. 166.
[35] *Federation and Unity in Italy,* 1862.

that the first measure of reform to be made in public law is the re-establishment of the Italian, Greek, Batavian [the Netherlands], Scandinavian and Danubian confederations as a prelude to the decentralization of the large States, followed by a general disarmament. In these conditions all nations would recover their freedom, and the notion of the balance of power in Europe would become a reality. This has been envisaged by all political writers and statesmen but has remained impossible so long as the great powers are centralized States.

It is not surprising that the notion of Federation should have been lost amid the splendors of the great States, since it is by nature peaceful and mild and plays a self-effacing role on the political scene.

(1863) *Fed.* pp. 335–36

Let us therefore postulate the following principle, which is based on fact as well as on reason: the strength of unity in any organism is in inverse ratio to its size. Consequently, in all collectivities the organic force loses in intensity what it gains in size, and vice versa . . . .

Let us apply this law to politics. The State is essentially one, indivisible and inviolable. The larger its population and territory, the weaker governmental unity must become. If not, it will become tyrannical and finally break down altogether. Even if branches or colonies are established nearby, sooner or later these branches or colonies will turn into new States, which will maintain only federal links with the parent State, or perhaps no links at all.

Nature itself sets us the example. When the fruit is ripe it breaks off and forms a new organism. When the young man reaches maturity he leaves his father and his mother, as the book of Genesis tells us, and cleaves unto his wife. When the new State is in a position to support itself, it declares its own independence. What right has the parent State to claim it as a vassal or as something to be exploited or possessed?

(1863–64)   *Pol. Contrads.* pp. 229–30

VIII   THE COLLECTIVE FORCE

Every human group—be it family, workshop, or battalion —can be regarded as an embryo society, and thus its force can to a certain extent form the basis of political power.

Usually, however, the city or State is not born of groups as I have just considered them. The State comes into being through the joining together of several groups whose nature and aims are different, each one having been formed for a specific function and to create a specific product. These groups then bind themselves together under a common law and in a common interest. It is a higher kind of collectivity in which each group, taken individually, helps to create a new force that will become greater as more functions are associated with it in ever more perfect harmony, and as the citizens become more completely involved.

To sum up, it is the relationship between the different parts that produces power in society and is the reality of the society itself. It is the same for the force in any body, whether organized or not, and this constitutes its reality. Let us imagine a society in which there were no longer any relationships between individuals and in which everyone provided for his own subsistence in complete isolation. However great the friendship between these men and however close they were, they would never be more than a number of individuals, and they would lose all reality and force. They would be like a body in which the particles had ceased to cohere and which would crumble into dust at the slightest shock.

QUESTION:

In the industrial group the collective force is quite clearly visible; it appears in the increase in production. But how can it be recognized within the political group? How does it differ from the force of ordinary groups? What is its distinctive product and what are its effects?

ANSWER:

The common people have always taken military strength, the building of monuments and public works to be signs of social force. But it is clear from what has just been said that these things, however large-scale they may be, are simply the result of ordinary collective force. It does not matter whether the groups of producers subsidized by the State are working in the service of the prince or for themselves. It is not here that we must look for signs of social power.

Since the active groups which make up the city differ in organization, aim and object, the link between them is not so much one of co-operation as of commutation. Thus the social force is essentially commutative in nature, but this does not mean that it is any less real.

(1858)   *Justice* II pp. 258–59

The view held in the ancient world about the nature and origins of social power is a witness to its truth. Just as attraction is immanent in matter and Justice immanent in man's heart, so power is immanent in society . . . .

This the earliest peoples felt intuitively, although they expressed it in mystical terms, attributing the origins of social power to the gods who fathered their dynasties. Their simple intelligence, which was more reliable than their senses, refused to believe that society, the State, and the power present in it were simply abstractions, although these things were intangible.

This is something the philosophers failed to see when

they said that the State was born of man's free will, or rather, of the abdication of his liberty. They were thus destroying by their dialectic the views religion had so patiently established.

(1858)   *Justice* II pp. 261–62

Because of the way the family is constituted, the father is naturally invested with the ownership and control of the force produced by the family group. This force is very soon increased by the additional labor of slaves and mercenaries, and in turn it increases their numbers. The family becomes the tribe and the father, whose status is maintained, finds that his power increases proportionately. This is the way that all similar forms of appropriation begin. Wherever there is a group of men or a collective force, there a class of patricians and nobles is formed.

When several families or concerns join together and form a city, the presence of a superior force immediately becomes apparent and is coveted by all. Who is to become its depositary, its beneficiary or its agent? Usually it is the head of the family whose sphere of influence embraces the largest number of children, relatives, allies, connections, slaves, paid workers, beasts of burden, capital and land; in a word, the man with the greatest collective force at his disposal. It is a natural law that a greater force absorbs and assimiliates lesser forces, and that domestic power constitutes a claim to political power. Thus the struggle for the crown is restricted to those who are strong . . . .

Furthermore, the alienation of the collective force, apart from the fact that it was the result of ignorance, seems to have been a method of preparing the races. It is very probable that the process of fitting primitive, savage man to social existence required a long period of refining body and soul. The educating of mankind was a process of mutual instruction and it was in the nature of things for the teachers to enjoy certain privileges. In the future, equality will be such that each man can in turn be both teacher and taught . . . .

Civilization sees to it that families and individuals who are in any case unequal in importance because of the accidents of fortune, become more markedly so once the collective forces have been appropriated and public power converted into privilege. Society is built upon hierarchies. The religion of the dynasty and the oath of allegiance to the emperor are expressions of this. In this system, the rule is that Justice, or what is termed Justice, always favors the superior rather than the inferior. While this appears to be an autocracy ordained by fate, it is in fact instability itself.

Sadly, everyone connives with the prince, since the spirit of equality created in man by Justice has been neutralized by the contrary prejudice, which is rendered ineradicable by the alienation of all collective force.

(1858) *Justice* II pp. 266–67, 269

Insofar as we may judge from its principal ideas and most genuine aspirations, in a democratic constitution politics and economics are one and the same thing, established on a single principle, that of mutuality. Just as, through a series of mutualist transactions, we have seen the great economic institutions emerge one after the other to form this vast human organism hitherto unimaginable, so the machinery of government in turn results not from some fictitious agreement, thought up to satisfy the republic and withdrawn as soon as it has been made, but from a real contract in which, instead of being absorbed into a central majesty, both personal and mystical, the individual sovereignty of the contracting parties acts as a positive guarantee of the liberty of States, communes and individuals.

We have then, not an abstract sovereignty of the people

as in the Constitution of 1793 and subsequent constitutions, or as in Rousseau's *Social Contract*, but an effective sovereignty of the working, reigning, governing masses. This is seen in welfare organizations, then in chambers of commerce, guilds of arts and crafts, and workingmen's associations, in exchanges and markets, academies and schools, agricultural associations, and finally in electoral meetings, parliamentary assemblies and the Councils of State, in the National Guard and even in churches and chapels. In all places and all cases the same *collective force* is at work acting for and through the principle of mutuality, which is the ultimate affirmation of the rights of man and of the citizen.

In this the working masses are truly, positively and effectively sovereign. Indeed, how could it be otherwise if they are in charge of the whole economic system including labor, capital, credit, property and wealth?

(1865)   *Pol. Cap.* pp. 215–16

The democratic ideal is that the masses who are governed should at the same time govern, and that society should be the same thing as the State, and the people the same thing as the government, just as in political economy, producers and consumers are the same thing. Of course I do not deny that different types of governmental organization have their own particular merits in particular circumstances and from the point of view of the government itself. If the State were never larger than a city or commune, I would allow each person to judge its form for himself, and that would be the end of the matter. But we must not forget that we are dealing with vast regions in which towns, villages and hamlets run into the thousands. All our statesmen, whatever their school of thought, think they can govern and control them according to the laws of patriarchy, conquest and property. By virtue of the very law of unity, I declare that this is impossible.

E

I must insist on the importance of the following observation which in politics is paramount.

Wherever men, together with their wives and children, gather together in one place, dwell together and cultivate their land in common, developing between them various industries, establishing relations of neighborliness, and, whether they like it or not, making themselves mutually dependent, they form what I call a natural group. This will soon become a State or political organization which asserts its unity, its independence, its own life or self-movement (*autokinesis*) and its autonomy.

Groups of the same kind, at some distance from each other may have common interests. One can understand that they may see eye to eye, join together in association and through this mutual assurance form a larger group, but never that when they unite in order to guarantee their interests and to increase their wealth they should go so far as offering themselves up as a kind of self-sacrifice to this new Moloch. It is impossible to make such a sacrifice. All these groups, however they may consider themselves and whatever they may do, are States, that is, indestructible organisms. There may very well be a new kind of legal tie between them, namely, a contract of mutuality, but they can no more strip themselves of their sovereign independence than the member of a State, because he is a citizen, can lose the prerogatives of a free man, producer and property owner. All that such an enterprise would achieve would be the creating of an irreconcilable antagonism between the general sovereignty and each individual sovereignty. Authority would be set against authority. In a word, while thinking that one is strengthening unity, one would in fact be creating disunity.

(1863–64)   *Pol. Contrads.* pp. 237–38

Since everybody, in secret, reasons in the same way, the result in the first instance is that the public reason,[36] which is the sum of individual wills,[36] is in no way, either in form or content, different from individual wills. Thus the worlds of nature and society are both extensions of the individual self or accessories to its absolutism . . . .

The collective reason, and all that this entails, is quite different [from egotistic absolutism]. It sets up one absolute against another in order to be entirely rid of this incomprehensible element, and considers as real and legitimate only terms whose relationship is one of antagonism. Thus it produces a synthesis of ideas that are very different from, and often completely contrary to, those produced by the individual *self*.

For instance, it says that although the property owner still has absolute power, property when it is counterbalanced by property through the public reason becomes pure delegation. Credit, which is always based on the lender's interest, is transformed into mutuality, which demands no interest. Commerce, by definition speculative, becomes equal exchange. Government, which is authoritarian in essence, becomes a balance of forces. Labor, which is repugnant to the intelligence, becomes an exercise for the mind. Charity becomes law. Competition becomes joint action. The single unit becomes a series, etc., etc.

These changes, it must be pointed out, do not entail a condemnation of individualism. Rather, they depend on it. "Men, citizens, workers," says the collective reason,

---

[36] *La raison publique* and *les raisons particulières,* here and throughout this section of *Justice* III, pp. 251–70. In most cases the word "reason" has been kept rather than using the word "will," which would read better in English and is part of Proudhon's meaning, so as to convey the Kantian terminology being used here.

which is truly practical and concerned with justice, "remain yourselves. Preserve and develop your own personalities. Defend your interests, use your own ideas. Nurture your individual will whose excessive tyranny today does you so much harm . . . . Respect only the dictates of your collective reason, whose judgments cannot be your own since it has been freed from the absolute without which you would be merely shadows."

(1858)   *Justice* III pp. 251, 253

People want to discover the true, natural, rational social system, since none of those that have been tried so far has been able to stand up to the inner destructive process that inevitably undermines them all. The problem has constantly preoccupied social philosophers from Minos in mythology to the leader of the Icarians.[37] Since no one had any positive ideas of Justice, economics or social dynamics, nor of the conditions for philosophical certainty, society was taken to be some sort of monster. It was likened to some huge organism that was created according to a hierarchical pattern. This pattern, before there was any thing such as Justice, constituted the laws of society and the conditions of its existence. It was like an animal of some unknown species, but which was still thought to possess a head, a heart, a nervous system, teeth, feet and so on like any other animal. From this chimerical organism that everyone endeavored to identify, Justice was then deduced. That is to say, morality emerged from physiology, or, as would be said today, law from duty. Thus Justice was still external to consciousness, liberty was still subject to fatality, and mankind was still in a fallen state.

I destroyed these fanciful notions in advance by pre-

[37] Cf. footnote 63 below, p. 177.

senting the facts and principles which get rid of them once and for all.

On the subject of the substance and organization of the social body I demonstrated that the former lay in the surplus of effective force of the group over and above the sum of individual forces which compose the group. I formulated the law about this by explaining how it can be reduced to a balance of forces, services and products, thus making the social system into a series of checks and balances. As an organism, society, which is the moral body *par excellence,* is essentially different from the human body whose law is that physical nature must be subordinated. This is why society finds any notion of hierarchy repellant, as is clear if we think of the formula: "All men are by nature of equal dignity and must become equal in condition through labor and justice." . . . .

In fact it is not so much a system, in the usual sense of the word, as an order in which all relationships are relationships of equality; one in which there is no such thing as superiority or obedience, center of gravity or direction; one in which the only law is that everything should be subject to justice, that is to say, to equilibrium.

(1858) *Justice* III pp. 264–66

The agent of the collective reason is the same as that of the collective force. It is the group of workers and teachers, the industrial, learned or artistic society, the academy, school or municipality. It is the national assembly, the club, or the jury. In a word, it is any group of men who have come together to discuss ideas and search for what is just: *Ubicumque fuerint duo vel tres congregati in nomine meo, ibi sum in medio corum.*[38]

One must be careful of only one thing. That is, that

[38] "For where two or three are gathered together in my name, there am I in the midst of them": Matt. xviii, 20.

when the group is called upon to vote, it should not vote *as one man* as a result of one individual feeling having become generally accepted. This can only lead to large-scale fraud, as is evident in most popular judgments. In battle the rule is that one man should fight against one man. But to vote as one man is contrary to reason.

Instead let us lay down this principle: the impersonality of the public reason presupposes as principle, the greatest possible contradiction; as means, the greatest possible multiplicity. And it is only to guarantee this impersonality that it is appropriate to create a special magistrature in order to supervise debates and watch over opinion. Alas! how many times during the last sixty years have we not been forced to recognize the inanity of the public watchdog, when there is no official organ to represent it and to act in its name in the way that there is a Ministry authorized in the name of public safety to suppress offenses and crimes?

If our academies were true to their original spirit, if they had the slightest idea of their mission, if the hypocrisy of the transcendentalists[39] had not perverted their conscience as much as their intelligence, nothing would be easier than for them to undertake this high task of judging works of scholarship. It is no more difficult to distinguish legitimate reasoning from mystical or absolutist reasoning in a speech or in a book on history, economics, politics, morality or literature, than it is in physics or natural history.

(1858)   *Justice* III pp. 270–71

[39] That is, the post-Kantian German school of philosophy, particularly Fichte and Schelling, whom Proudhon had studied in Paris in the 1840s; cf. *Introduction*, p. 19. Proudhon's point here is that scientific knowledge must be freed of all mystical or religious doctrines.

What is universal suffrage, considered not from the point of view of its material functioning but from the point of view of its essence or idea? ... It is, in the nation, the power of society or force of the collectivity, which even in this rudimentary form is already functioning fully and exercising its sovereignty. It contains, like so many faculties in embryo, all the liberties, rights, guarantees and forms of progress that are the attributes of a free and civilized society. All institutions, all justice, and all organizations exist in potential within this parent institution, and anything that is not born of it normally and spontaneously, and particularly anything which impedes its growth, must be regarded as abortive and illegitimate. In short, universal suffrage provides us, on a reduced scale, or better still, in an embryonic state, with the complete system of future society. If it is reduced to the people nominating a few hundred deputies who have no initiative, and most of whom are elected on the recommendation of the Government, social sovereignty becomes a mere fiction and the Revolution is strangled at birth.

(1863)   *Democrats* p. 84

The masses are indeed unintelligent and blind. Why should it be shameful to admit it? It is in their nature, and I would even willingly say that it is their right. There is no doubt that they need a guiding principle. But where is that principle to come from? That is the real question. My reply is that the guiding principle of universal suffrage must come from universal suffrage itself as it functions in its own particular conditions and ways. Neither the Government nor anybody else has the right to prejudice this principle. The only persons who may legitimately advise the masses are those who express their opinions through the press or the spoken word. Thus the true guide of universal suffrage is this General Reason which is impersonal and synthesizing and which, being created from the clash of ideas, never fails to appear wherever man has the right to think, speak and write freely.

(1863)   *Democrats* p. 91

IX PROPERTY AND THE STATE

Property and Possession

If I had to answer the question "What is slavery?" and if I were to answer in one word, "Murder," I would immediately be understood. I would not need to use a lengthy argument to demonstrate that the power to deprive a man of his thoughts, his will and his personality is a power of life and death, and that to enslave a man is to murder him. Why then, to the question "What is property?" may I not likewise reply "theft," without knowing that I am certain to be misunderstood, even though the second proposition is simply a transformation of the first?[40]

(1840)   *Memoir* p. 131

[40] This is the statement that made Proudhon famous. Clear echoes are here of both Pascal and Rousseau (see W. Pickles' article in *Politica*, Vol. 3, no. 13, pp. 256–57; London, September, 1938). Pensée no. 295 (Brunschvicg edn.) on *Mine, thine* for example: " 'This dog is mine,' said those poor children; 'that is my place in the sun.' Here is the beginning and the image of the usurpation of all the earth." Or the opening sentence of Part 2 of the *Discourse on the Origin of Inequality:* "The first man who, having enclosed a piece of ground, bethought himself of saying, 'This is mine,' and found people simple enough to believe him, was the real founder of civil society," and of the "crimes, wars and murders" that followed on from this.

In my first two Memoirs, in a frontal attack on established order, I said, among other things: "Property is theft." My aim was to make a protest and, so to speak, to highlight the utter hollowness of our institutions.

(1863–64)   *Property* p. 37

What was the special target of my attack in 1840? It was the right of escheat or *aubaine*,[41] which is such an integral part of property that where it does not exist, neither does property.

(1863–64)   *Property* p. 20

Property is an enormous subject because it involves so many interests, arouses so much envy and awakens so many fears. Property is a very difficult word because of its many senses in our language, its ambiguities and the nonsensical meanings sometimes attached to it. Either through ignorance or through bad faith, no one has ever followed my lead on this subject. What, indeed, was to be expected when even jurists, law professors and Academy prize winners confuse PROPERTY with *possession* in its various forms: rent, tenant farming, long-lease, usufruct, and enjoyment of things subject to wear and tear. "What!" says one person, "am I not the owner of my furniture, my cloak and my hat that I have duly paid for?" "What," says another, "are then the wages that I have earned with the sweat of my brow not my property?" "I have invented a machine," cries someone else, "I have spent twenty years of my life on it in study, trial and research, and now my discovery is to be taken away—literally stolen—from me!" "And I have produced a book,"

---

[41] Cf. footnote 15 above.

E*

says yet another, "which is the result of long and patient reflection. My style is in it, my ideas, my very soul—all that marks one man off from another—and now I am told that I have no right to be paid for it!"

It was to that kind of would-be logic, and showing the absurd limits to which the confusion of the various meanings of the word *property* can be pushed, that I replied in 1863 in my *Majorats littéraires:*[42] "This word has many widely different meanings, and it would be ludicrous to pass without comment from one to another and yet appear to be discussing the same thing. . . .

In springtime poor peasant women pick strawberries in the woods and take them into the towns to sell. These strawberries are their produce, and therefore, as Abbé Pluquet[43] would say, their *property*. But is this really so? If it were, this would be equivalent to saying that they were the owners of the woods the strawberries came from. But alas, the contrary is true. If these strawberry-sellers were really the owners of the strawberries, they would not be going to the woods to pick fruit for the land-owners. They would be eating it themselves.". . . .

Has the reader already realized that hats and coats, estates and houses are owned in vastly different ways, and that although language may allow one by a kind of analogy to talk about a bed or a table as "property" just as one talks about a field as "property," jurisprudence does not allow this confusion? . . . .

---

[42] A collection of several of his essays on literary copyright, arguing against restrictions on publication, and discussing the relationship between art and industrialism.

[43] The Abbé Pluquet, 1716–90, became a professor at the Collège de France under Louis XVI, and published a *Philosophical and Political Treatise on Luxury* in 1786. Pluquet pleads for a life according to "nature", which has bountifully provided sufficient for all. The proprietor should be self-supporting; it is an argument in favor of the limitation rather than the abolition of property.

The reader now doubtless understands the difference between *possession* and PROPERTY. It was only the latter that I called theft. Property is the biggest problem of society today. It is the whole problem.

(1863–64)   *Property*[44] pp. 2–3, 6–7, 15

SUMMARY OF MY PREVIOUS WRITINGS ON PROPERTY

When in 1840 I published my first *Memoir on Property* [*What Is Property?*] I was careful to make a distinction between property and possession, the latter being no more than the right to make use of an object. In a society in which nobody has the right to misuse things, there is no right of property, only a right of possession. I still maintain today what I said in my first *Memoir:* the owner of a thing, be it land, house, instrument of labor, raw material or finished product, may be either one person or a group, the father of a family or a whole nation, but, whatever the case, he can be said to be the property owner on one condition only: he must have absolute sovereignty over it, he must be its exclusive master— *dominus,* it must be his domain—*dominium.*

---

[44] The *Theory of Property* was published posthumously. It was prepared by J. A. Langlois (an old friend and disciple of Proudhon) and others from Proudhon's own notes, which he had been working on during the last three years of his life. During this time Proudhon also completed *On the Political Capacity of the Working Classes.* The manuscript of the *Theory of Property* consists of Proudhon's own summary of his previous writings on the subject, which make up the second chapter (pp. 16–64) of the book: pp. 125–31 of the selections here. He had also worked out chapter headings for the rest of the book, but the material had not been arranged into chapters. Although (apart from the first part) the *Theory of Property* is not a completed work of Proudhon, it is generally accepted (e.g., by Aimé Berthod in *Proudhon and Property: a Socialism for the Peasants*) as the only complete presentation of Proudhon's views on the subject that first made his name as a revolutionary writer.

Now in 1840 I categorically rejected the notion of the right of property. Those who have read my first *Memoir* know that I rejected it for both the group and the individual, the nation and the citizen, and thus I was not advocating either communism or State ownership. I denied that there was a right of property, that is, the right to abuse anything at all, even to abuse what we call our faculties. Man has no more right to misuse his faculties than society has to misuse its power.

(1863–64)   *Property* p. 16

At that time [in 1840] I said that man, in his capacity of producer, undoubtedly has a personal right to the product of his labor. But what is this product? It is his shaping and working of the raw material. But that raw material itself is in no sense his creation. If therefore he was entitled to appropriate the raw material before he had added his labor to it, it cannot be in his capacity of producer that he did so. It must therefore have been in some other capacity.

(1863–64)   *Property* p. 17

I quite see that, as in Victor Cousin's[45] argument, the personal right to possess the work added to the raw material entails also a personal right of possession over the material worked upon. But does this correspond to the facts?

Wherever there is no shortage of land, where any man can have access to it as and when he pleases, I accept the

[45] Victor Cousin, 1792–1867, French philosopher who was a professor at the *École normale,* member of the French Academy and of Louis-Philippe's cabinet for a time. Proudhon is referring here to part of Victor Cousin's argument in *Cours d'histoire de la philosophie morale* against Hobbes in favor of absolute property rights.

principle of the exclusive right of the first occupier. But I accept it only provisionally. Wherever conditions are different, I accept only equal division. Anything else, in my view, is an abuse. I quite agree that the man who first plowed up the land should receive compensation for his labor. What I cannot accept, regarding land, is that the work put in gives a right to ownership of what has been worked on . . . .

Simple justice, I said in my first *Memoir*, requires that equal division of land shall not operate only at the outset. If there is to be no abuse, it must be maintained from generation to generation. This applies to all extractive industries. As for workers engaged in other industries, they must receive the same as others for equal work. Without actually owning the land, they must have free use of the raw materials they need for their industries. By paying with their own labor, or, to put it another way, with their products, for what the landowners provide, they must pay only for any work that the latter may have added to the raw material. Labor must be paid for only by labor and the raw material must be free. If the landowners derive an income for themselves, this is an abuse.

(1863–64)   *Property* pp. 18–19

If we disregard the liberty of the cultivator, which in any case is only limited when he is no more than a tenant farmer, it is one of the antinomies or anti-laws[46] of landed property that the idle landlord nevertheless becomes an agent of natural justice in his relationship to the farmer. How does he do this? Firstly, by claiming from the farmer, for the duration of the lease, the rent to which really he is no more entitled than any other citizen. Secondly, by denying to the farmer any surplus value that his labor

[46] *Contre-lois,* a neologism of Proudhon, modeled on *contre-sens.*

may have given to the property and that he—the farmer—
would be tempted to claim for himself.

Has not the tenant farmer who agrees to pay a certain
annual rent to the landowner calculated in advance the
various expenses that his work will entail during his ten-
ancy? Has he not calculated that the market price of his
crops will completely amortize his expenses as well as
provide him with a fair recompense for his labor? I admit
that the landowner, not having had to meet these expenses,
yet finding himself on the expiration of the lease with
improved land that brings him a higher income through
no work of his own, has no more right than the tenant
farmer to profit from the surplus value. And I confess that
if I were forced to choose between the idle landlord and
the hard-working tenant farmer I would not hesitate to
declare myself in favor of the latter. But the tenant farmer
who has calculated correctly has no greater right to the
surplus value that has accrued to the land as the result
of his labor than if it had been produced by society
through the growth of the population or the opening of
a new road, bridge, canal or railway. The idle landlord has
certainly no right to retain the surplus value for himself,
but he is performing an act of justice when he takes it
away from the tenant farmer, who has in any case been
paid for his labor by society.

Thus I said in 1846 in my *System of Economic Contradictions* "that property follows in the wake of labor to
take away everything over and above the value of the
labor actually expended in making the product . . . .

Rent is therefore in its nature and essence an agent of
distributive justice, one of the countless methods by which
the inherent genius of the economic mechanism promotes
equality . . . .

For the mechanism inherent in society does not operate
as our theorizers do, through sterile abstraction ... Its
ideas become persons and things. It works through a series
of concrete embodiments, and in moving toward the or-

ganizations of society it relies always on the individual
... Men had to be bound to the land, so the spirit of society created property. Then it became necessary to know
who owned what throughout the world. Instead of loudly
proclaiming a collective operation, the spirit of society set
individual interests at odds, and from the strife between
the exploiter of the land and its owner, there emerged
the form of settlement that was best for society."

(1863–64)   *Property* pp. 32–35

My aim here is to consolidate the whole of my earlier
criticism of property, leading up to the proof of the thesis
that if property is to be accepted, this can be done only
by accepting also the principles of *Immanent Justice,
Sovereignty of the Individual* and *Federation.*

(1863–64)   *Property* p. 64

NEW THEORY OF PROPERTY

It is neither in its basic principle, nor its origins, nor
its physical nature that we must look for the justification
of property. In all these respects, I repeat, property has
no more to offer than possession. Its justification is in its
AIMS . . . .
The only thing we know with any certainty about property that distinguishes it from possession is that it is absolute and unjust. And it is precisely in these things, its
absolute nature and the abuses—to use no stronger term—
to which it gives rise, that we must look for the nature of
its aims.

(1863–64)   *Property* pp. 128, 129

When I say that the aims of property, the way it functions, and consequently its justification must be sought for
in its abuses, let it be clearly understood that in so saying

I do not see myself as glorifying these abuses, which in themselves are bad and which everyone wants to abolish. I mean that because property is absolute, subject to no restrictions and therefore undefinable, its purpose, if it has one, and its function, if it is true that it is a part of the social organism, can be discovered only by studying its abuses. When its function is known and its justification proved by its purpose, then we can try to discover ways of eliminating the abuses.

(1863–64)   *Property* pp. 154–55

All citizens have the same rights and the same dignity within the State. If nature created them with unequal creative faculties, it is in the nature of civilization and laws to limit the effects of this inequality in practice by giving everybody the same guarantees and, as far as possible, the same education. But property obstructs this desirable process by its constant transfers and monopolizations. As a result, property is seen as an obstacle to equality and is ranked in this respect lower than possession.

The abuse thus pointed out certainly exists. God forbid that I should fail to recognize it since it is in the abuses of property that I am trying to discover its organic function and the ends to which it is destined by Providence. But, surprising as this may be, the criticism of property as an obstacle to equality of condition and fortune could far more justly be leveled at fief and possession because they seem to have been created with exactly opposite aims and intentions. It is a fact of universal history that land has been no more unequally divided than in places where the system of possession alone has predominated and where fief has taken the place of freehold. Likewise, States in which the most liberty and equality are to be found are those where property reigns.

(1863–64)   *Property* p. 146

Property must be spread and consolidated, under pain of falling back into State control and thereby launching society once again on a career of revolution and catastrophe. To return once more to the fundamental idea in this work—this is how property, by creating guarantees for itself that both spread it more equally and establish it more firmly in society, itself becomes a guarantee of liberty and keeps the State on an even keel. Once property has been firmly established, given a moral basis, and surrounded by protective, or more accurately, emancipating institutions, the power of the State is increased to the maximum but it is nevertheless the citizens who remain at the helm. Politics becomes a science, or, better still, a form of Justice. Private interests become identical with public interests, and every citizen is able to make his own judgment on the business situation and the functioning of government through the repercussions that these have on his property and his industry.

(1863–64)   *Property* p. 189

Property is by nature totally indifferent to the structure of power whether it be monarchic, democratic, aristocratic, constitutional or despotic. What it wants is for the State, the body politic, to be under its control, and for government to function through it and for it, at its pleasure and for its profit . . . . Above all, government must be property's creature and slave, or it will be destroyed. No power can withstand it; it holds no dynasty sacred, no constitution inviolable . . . .

We know what happened during the French Revolution: forced sale or confiscation of a third of the land, its conversion into holdings free of feudal dues—which indeed were abolished. The law of primogeniture was abolished.

Unsold fiefs were converted into freehold estates. This is what made France a democracy.

In 1799, property in its new guise proclaimed itself in a *coup d'état* and abolished the Republic. Fourteen years later, displeased with the Emperor who had held it in check, it abandoned Napoleon and put an end to Imperial rule. It was property that in 1830 caused the downfall of Charles X, and in 1848, that of Louis-Philippe. The haute bourgeoisie or large-property owners were divided, the middle class or small-property owners were ready to rise. It was a handful of Republicans, followed by a few of the common people, who settled the matter. Once Louis-Philippe was out of the way, power should logically have passed into the hands of the Republicans. But logic does not always prevail. Property, which for a moment had been taken unawares, soon reappeared and overthrew the Republic for the second time. Since the common people had nothing, democracy was founded on a void. The *coup d'état* of December 2, like that of the 18th *Brumaire*,[47] was successful because it was backed by property. Louis-Napoleon simply anticipated the desires of the bourgeoisie, and was doubly certain of success since the common people saw him as their protector against bourgeois exploitation.

Thus it is clear that property in itself owes allegiance to no particular form of government, and is bound by no dynastic or legal ties. Its politics may be summed up in a single word: exploitation, or even anarchy. It is the most formidable enemy and most treacherous ally of any form of power. In short, in its relation to the State it is governed by only one principle, one sentiment, one concern: self-interest, or egoism . . . .

This is why all governments, all utopias and all Churches distrust property, not to mention Lycurgus and

[47] December 2, 1851, brought Napoleon III to power; 18th *Brumaire*, 1799, brought Napoleon I to power.

Plato, who banned property—like poetry—from their republics, or the Caesars, popular leaders who conquered
only to obtain property, and attacked the civil rights of
citizens as soon as they had become dictators . . . .

 In the light of all these facts we can conclude that property is the greatest existing revolutionary force, with
an unequaled capacity for setting itself against authority . . . .

Even if it has the most rational Constitution and is ex-
tremely liberal and well intentioned, the State is over-
whelmingly powerful and capable of destroying everything around it if it is not counterbalanced by some other
force. What other force is available? The whole strength
of the State lies in the support it receives from its citizens.
The State is the uniting of all general interests. It is supported by the general will and can be backed by the united
strengths of all its members. What force could adequately
counterbalance the enormous power of the State? There
is only one: property. The combined forces of property
would indeed constitute a power equal to that of the
State. It might be asked why possession or feudal
ownership by fief could not serve as a counterweight.
The reason is that possession and fief are State institutions, and thus because each is an integral part of the
State they cannot oppose the State, but rather support it.
Their weight is on the same side of the balance, so they
cannot produce an equilibrium but can only add more
weight to the governing power . . . .

If one force is to compel respect from another force,
each must be independent of the other. They must be two
distinct forces, not one. If, therefore, the citizen is to count
for anything in the State, personal freedom is not enough.
His individuality, like that of the State, must be founded
on something material over which he must have sovereign
possession, just as the State has sovereign possession over
public property. Private property provides this foundation.

The principal function of private property within the

political system will be to act as a counterweight to State power, and by so doing to insure the liberty of the individual. If this function is suppressed, or, to put it another way (tantamount to the same thing), if property is no longer as absolute as we have seen it to be, if this is no longer its distinguishing feature, if restrictions are imposed upon it and it is declared untransferable or indivisible, then it immediately loses its strength and no longer carries any weight. It reverts to being simply a benefice, or a precarious tenure. It is a feudal dependency of the government, powerless to act against it.

There is therefore a conflict between the absolute right of the State and the absolute right of the property owner.

(1863–64)   *Property* pp. 131, 134–38

Property was not created by law. It was not decreed by an assembly of representatives, deciding after lengthy deliberation and in full knowledge of the facts. It is produced spontaneously by society, the expression of a self-confident will that makes itself felt in the individual and in the masses alike.

Let us note the fundamental reason for property's being created in this way. Human consciousness, guided by the wisdom of the nations, demands that certain things should be totally and completely free and reject any kind of control. Love, art and labor are among these things and to their number we must add property . . . .

Property must be in the same position as love, labor and art. That is not to say that the property owner must imagine that he may go beyond the bounds of reason and restraint. However absolute the law makes him, he will soon learn to his cost that property cannot live by abuse and that it too must bow to common sense and morality. He will learn that if the absolute aspires to leave the domain of metaphysics and to become tangible reality, it can accomplish this only through reason and justice. If ever the absolute moves toward realization, it becomes accountable to knowledge and law. Since, however, it is essential to the progress of justice that the conformity of property to truth and morality should come willingly and that the property owner be his own master, no obligations will be imposed on him by the State. This is in complete accord with our principles. For the aim of civilization, as we have said, and the task of the State is to allow each individual to exercise the right to administer his own justice and to become an instrument of right and agent of the law. This will lead to the abolition of written constitutions and statutes. The principle that governs property is that there should be the smallest possible number of laws, that is to say, the smallest possible number of prescribed regulations and official statutes; it is a principle of evident moral superiority, the only one by which the free man can be distinguished from the slave.

In the system brought in by the Revolution of 1789 and which was sanctioned by our French Codes the citizen is more than just a free man. He is part of the sovereign. His sovereignty is exercised not only at primary meetings or in the assemblies of his representatives, but also and above all through his industry, through the use to which he puts his mind, and in the administration of his property. In this sphere the legislator intended that the citizen should, at his own risk, enjoy the greatest possible autonomy and be held responsible for his actions only when they are injurious to third parties, to society or to the State considered as a third party. The Revolutionary legislator believed that only in these conditions could society flourish and follow in the paths of prosperity and justice. He got rid of all feudal fetters and restrictions. This is why the citizen, in his social function as worker, producer or possessor, is in no sense a functionary of the State. He is dependent upon no one, does as he pleases, and disposes of his intelligence, his hands, his capital and his land as he sees fit. And history shows that in countries where there is this industrial autonomy and where the rights of property are thus absolute, there also is the greatest wealth and virtue.

(1863–64)   *Property* pp. 162–65

In what does property or civil ownership differ from possession? In two things, neither of which by itself seems to me to contradict either law or morality. The first is that the property owner is answerable to neither prince nor commune, only to himself. The second is that his authority as head of the family is self-generating and creates no responsibility to anybody.

(1863–64)   *Property* p. 111

It is in political systems based on elections that the action of property is most strikingly apparent. Not only has the State lost its right to confiscate property, but it also has had to stoop to asking the property owner periodically to renew its tenure of office. For this is what happens at parliamentary elections. While we are on the subject, much has been said against the principle that makes property-owning the proof of political ability, and against a regime that denied such men as Rousseau, Lamennais and Béranger the right to vote while granting it to all the Prudhommes, Jourdains, Dandins and Gérontes.

The February Revolution [of 1848] abolished electoral property qualifications in favor of universal suffrage. But still the democratic purists were not satisfied: some wanted to give the vote to children and women and others objected to the exclusion of bankrupts, prisoners and freed convicts. It would have been only a short step to giving the vote to horses and donkeys.

The theory of property as I am presenting it gets rid of all such nebulous ideas. According to this theory, property is not a proof or guarantee of political capability. Political capacity is a faculty of intelligence and conscience and has nothing to do with the owning of property. It is fair to say that everybody agrees on this point. But I would add that, though it is true that opposition to despotism is an act of conscience that can happen whether or not the citizen pays two hundred or five hundred francs in taxes and has an income of more than three thousand francs, it is nevertheless also true that for this opposition to be considered as a collective protest that will carry some weight against the power of the State it must express the will of a body of property owners. This is simply the way things work and has nothing to do with the capability or civic sense of the citizens . . . .

An elector's vote is of no real value—I am not discussing moral value—against authority unless it represents a real force, and property is that force. To return, then, to universal suffrage and the question of non-property-owning voters. There are two alternatives. Either they will vote with the property owners, in which case they will be of no use, or they will dissociate themselves from them. In this latter case, the State will remain in control whether it seeks support in the mass of the electorate, sides with the property owners, or stands between the two to act as a mediator and imposes its arbitration. Giving political rights to the people was not in itself a bad idea; what was wrong was that first of all they should have been given property.

(1863–64) *Property* pp. 152–54

The truth as I see it is that both property and the State are absolutes, destined to confront each other, just as the property owner is destined to confront his neighboring property owner. And it is the confrontation of these two absolutes that generates political activity and social life just as the opposition of two electric currents sparks the motor force of lightning that gives light and life.

(1863–64)　*Property* p. 193

In my *System of Economic Contradictions* [of 1846], I reiterated and confirmed my first definition of property and then added another, quite contrary one based on considerations of quite a different kind. But this neither destroyed nor was destroyed by my first argument. This new definition was: property is liberty. Property is theft; property is liberty: these two propositions stand side by side in my *System of Economic Contradictions* and each is shown to be true.

(1863–64)　*Property* p. 37

Property in its modern form, which appears to be founded, in defiance of any notion of right and good sense, on a double absolutism, may in fact be considered as a triumph of Liberty. For it is born of Liberty, not, as it may at first appear, against right, but through the operation of a much better understanding of right. What, indeed, is Justice other than an equal balance of forces? Justice is not merely a relationship, an abstract idea, a fictitious creation of the intelligence or an act of faith on the part of conscience. It is something real and all the more imperative because based on those freely moving forces that we know to be realities.

There is a corollary to this principle that property is the only power that can act as a counterweight to the State, because it shows no reverence to princes, rebels against society and is, in short, anarchist. The corollary is that property, an absolutism within an absolutism, is also an element of division within the State. State power is the kind of power that absorbs everything else into it. If it is allowed to take its own way, all individuality will quickly disappear, swallowed up by the collectivity, and society will sink into communism. Property, on the contrary, is a decentralizing force. Being itself absolute, it is anti-despotic and anti-unitary. Property is the basis of any system of federation. This is why property, which is by nature autocratic, automatically becomes democratic when it forms part of an ordered political society.

(1863–64)   Property p. 144

According to whether we judge property by its principle or by its aims, it can appear either as the most arrant and cowardly of immoralities or as the very ideal of civic and domestic virtue.

Consider first its vulgar countenance that shows no spark of genius, love or honor. Its eyes squint, its smile is treacherous and its brow is ignorant of shame. Its features are hard, its jaws formidable—but they are the jaws of a hippopotamus, not a lion. The whole visage seems to say: "Nothing is of any account except owning property and owning enough of it, whatever the means by which it was acquired." The owner of this face is not so crass as to believe that property is in itself a merit. But he attaches no importance to merit since he is persuaded that nobility, bravery, industry, talent, integrity and all the things that men esteem are nothing without property, and that he who can say: "I own" can very well do without the rest. He will not argue with you about the origins or the lawfulness of property. Secretly he is inclined to believe that originally property was a usurpation that has now been conveniently forgotten by the law. But since, as he sees it, what was worth beginning is worth continuing, his sole aim (with due respect to the police!) is to increase the amount of property he owns by all the questionable means by which he got it in the first place. He exploits the poor, haggles with the laborer over his wages, pillages and pilfers on all sides, here appropriating a furrow from his neighbor's field and there moving the boundary stones when he is sure that he will not be seen. I have even seen one such man in a boundary ditch, scraping up the earth with his bare hands and throwing it onto his own side, and looking as if he were eating and enjoying it! He makes it his business to extract the maximum from savings and interest. There is no harsher usurer, no worse employer, no one slower to pay his bills. On top of all this, he is a hypocrite and a coward, afraid of the devil and of the law, fearing the penalty rather than opinion. Judging others by his own standards he sees them all as rogues. He is completely indifferent to public affairs and never becomes involved in politics except to get his taxes reduced or to sell his vote, while he rejoices in the electoral incorruptibility of his farsighted fellow citizens that allows him to turn his own vote to advantage. Such is the property owner as seen literally and through the eyes of principle—or through those of materialism and egoism, which is another way of saying the same thing.

Let us now look at the other side of the picture. There we find a face that shows candor and noble sentiments. What particularly distinguishes this person is that, in his guilelessness, the idea of property would never have occurred to him. He would have protested with all the energy the conscience can command against the establishment of this institution based on absolutism and abuse. Out of respect for people's rights and in the interest of the masses he would have upheld the classical practice of possession. And quite unwittingly, striving for the exact opposite, he would have perpetuated despotism within the State and servitude within society. Today property exists, and the accident of birth has made such a man a property owner. He possesses without being possessed and believes in the rightness of a principle that he in no way desired and for which we must all accept responsibility. But he holds at the same time that property entails obligations. Though the law demands nothing of him, his conscience demands everything. He is the hardest of workers, the guardian of law and liberty. For him the life of the property owner is not that of a pleasure-seeking parasite, but one of struggle. In ancient Rome, playing the triple role of priest, judge and captain, noble toiler and austere head of the family, he immortalized and gave all the glory of sovereignty to the name that today is held almost in ridicule: that of CITIZEN. In 1789 he took up arms against feudal despotism and against the foreigner. Conscripted soldiers have now taken the place of the battalions of volunteers, but if the armies of the Empire rivaled those of the Republic in courage, they remain inferior to them in virtue. While he waits for the equality that will come with progress, he remains the friend of the laboring people, but never their flatterer.

In 1848 it was he who said that the aim of democracy was not to shorten dress coats but to lengthen jackets. And finally he tries to protect contemporary society against the assaults of unbridled industrialism, corrupt literature, garrulous demagogy, faithless Jesuitism and unprincipled politics. Such is the property owner according to the aims of property. We may also call him the property owner according to the spirit.

(1863–64)   Property pp. 168–71

PART TWO

The Progress of
the Revolution

X CORRESPONDENCE BETWEEN PROUDHON AND MARX[48]

Marx to Proudhon

Brussels, May 5, 1846

My Dear Proudhon,

I very often intended to write to you since I left Paris, but circumstances independent of my will have hitherto prevented me from doing so. Let me assure you that the only reason for my silence has been that I was overwhelmed with work and kept busy by the troubles involved in a change of residence, and the like.

And now let us jump in *medias res!* Together with two friends of mine, Frederick Engels and Philippe Gigot (both in Brussels), I have organized a continuous correspondence with the German Communists and Socialists, which is to take up both the discussion of scientific questions and the supervision of popular publications as well as socialist propaganda, which can be carried on in Germany by this means. It will be the chief aim of our correspondence, however, to put the German Socialists in contact with the French and English Socialists; to keep the foreigners posted on the socialist movements that are going to take place in Germany, and to inform the Germans in Germany of the progress of socialism in France and England. In this way it will be possible to air differences of opinion. An exchange of ideas will ensue and impartial criticism be secured. It is a step which the

[48] Cf. *Introduction,* p. 18.

social movement should take in its *literary* expression in order to free itself of its *national* limitations. And at the time for action it is certainly of great benefit to everyone to be enlightened on the state of affairs abroad as well as at home.

Besides the Communists in Germany our correspondence would also embrace the German Socialists in Paris and London. Our connections with England have already been established; as for France, we are all of the opinion that we could not find a better correspondent there than you. As you know, the English and Germans have up to the present appreciated you more than your own fellow countrymen.

So you see, it is only a question of initiating a regular correspondence and of assuring it the facilities for following the social movement in the various countries, a question of making it interesting, meaty and varied, which the work of a single individual can never achieve.

If you accept our proposal, postage for the letters sent by us to you and by you to us will be paid for here, the money raised in Germany being intended to cover the expenses of the correspondence.

The address we would ask you to write to here is that of M. Philippe Gigot, 8, rue Bodenbrock. He is also the one to sign the letters from Brussels.

I need not add that the utmost secrecy must be maintained by you with regard to the whole of this correspondence; in Germany our friends have to act with the greatest circumspection to avoid compromising themselves.

Send us an early reply and believe in the sincere friendship of

Your humble servant,
Karl Marx

Brussels. May 5, 1846

P.S. Let me here denounce M. Grün in Paris. The man is nothing more than a literary swindler, a charlatan, who would like to deal in modern ideas. He tries to cover up his ignorance with high-flown, arrogant phrases, but he has only succeeded in making himself look ridiculous through his pompous nonsense. Moreover, the man is *dangerous*. He *abuses* the relations that his impertinence has enabled him to establish with well-known authors, using them as a ladder and compromising them in the eyes of the German public. In his book on the French socialists he dares to call himself Proudhon's tutor (*Privatdozent*, an academic rank in Germany), claims to have revealed important principles of German knowledge to him, and jokes about his writings. Therefore beware of this parasite. Perhaps I will mention this individual to you again later.

I am happy to have this opportunity of telling you how pleased I am to enter into relations with someone as distinguished as yourself. Meanwhile, allow me to sign myself,

> Your humble servant,
> *Philippe Gigot*

For my part I can only hope that you will approve of the project which we have just proposed to you and that you will be obliging enough not to deny us your cooperation. May I say that your writings have left me with the greatest respect for you and that I remain

> Your humble servant,
> *Frederic Engels*

Proudhon to Marx

Lyon, May 17, 1846.

My dear Monsieur Marx,

I willingly agree to become one of the stages of your correspondence, whose aims and organization appear to be most useful. However, I do not promise to write to you either at length or often since my various occupations as well as my natural laziness do not allow me to make these epistolary efforts. I will also take the liberty of making several reservations which have been prompted by various passages in your letter.

Firstly, although my ideas on matters of organization and realization are at the moment quite settled, at least as far as principles are concerned, I believe that it is my duty, and that it is the duty of all socialists, to maintain for some time yet an attitude of criticism and doubt. In short, I profess with the public an almost total anti-dogmatism in economics.

By all means let us work together to discover the laws of society, the ways in which these laws are realized and the process by which we are able to discover them. But, for God's sake, when we have demolished all *a priori* dogmas, do not let us think of indoctrinating the people in our turn. Do not let us fall into your compatriot Martin Luther's inconsistency. As soon as he had overthrown Catholic theology he immediately, with constant recourse to excommunications and anathemas, set about founding a Protestant theology. For three hundred years Germany's whole concern has been to destroy Luther's hodgepodge. Let us not make further work for humanity by creating another shambles. I wholeheartedly applaud your idea of bringing all shades of opinion to light. Let us have a good and honest polemic. Let us set the world an example of wise and farsighted tolerance, but simply because we are leaders of a movement let us not instigate a new intolerance. Let us not set ourselves up as the apostles of a new religion, even if it be the religion of logic or of reason. Let us welcome and encourage all protests, let us get rid of all exclusiveness and all mysticism. Let us never consider any question exhausted, and when we have used our very last argument, let us begin again, if necessary, with eloquence and irony. On this condition I will join your association with pleasure, otherwise I will not.

I must also make some observations about the phrase in your letter, "at the time for action." Perhaps you still hold the opinion that no reform is possible without a helping *coup de main,* without what used to be called a revolution but which is quite simply a jolt. I confess that my most recent studies have led me to abandon this view, which I understand and would willingly discuss, since for a long time I held it myself. I do not think that this is what we need in order to succeed, and consequently we must not suggest *revolutionary* action as the means of social reform because this supposed means would simply be an appeal to force and to arbitrariness. In brief, it would be a contradiction. I put the problem in this way: *How can we put back into society, through some system of economics, the wealth which has been taken out of society by another system of economics?* In other words, through Political Economy we must turn the theory of Property against Property in such a way as to create what you German socialists call *community* and which for the moment I will only go so far as calling *liberty* or *equality.* Now I think I know the way in which this problem may be very quickly solved. Therefore I would rather burn Property little by little than give it renewed strength by making a Saint Bartholomew's Day of property owners.

My next work, which at present is in the middle of being printed, will explain this to you further.[49]

---

[49] That is, *System of Economic Contradictions or the Philosophy of Poverty,* which Marx attacked in French by writing *The Poverty of Philosophy.*

This, my dear philosopher, is my present position. I may be mistaken, and if that happens and you give me the cane, I would cheerfully endure it while waiting for my revenge.[50] I must add in passing that this also seems to be the feeling of the French working class. Our proletarians are so thirsty for knowledge that they would receive us very badly if all we could give them to drink were blood. To be brief, it would in my opinion be very bad policy to use the language of extermination. Rigorous measures will come right enough; in this the people are in no need of exhortation.

I sincerely regret the minor divisions which would appear to exist already in German socialism and of which your complaint against M. Grün gives me proof. I am rather afraid that you may have seen this writer in a false light, and I appeal, M. Marx, to your well-balanced judgment. Grün is in exile with no fortune, with a wife and two children and with no source of income but his pen. What else besides modern ideas could he exploit in order to make a living? I understand your philosophic wrath and I agree that the holy writ of humanity should never be used as a bargaining counter. But in this case I must consider the misfortune, the extreme necessity, and I excuse the man. Ah yes, if we were all millionaires things would be much better. We should all be saints and angels. But we must *live*, and you know that this word is still far

---

[50] Proudhon did consider writing a rejoinder to Marx's attack on him, and Proudhon's copy of the *Poverty of Philosophy* is annotated as if in preparation for a reply. In his diary there are several references showing how Proudhon had been stung by Marx's "cane"; the entry for September 23, 1847, calls Marx "the tapeworm of socialism." Probably the 1848 Revolution turned Proudhon's mind to other matters than replying to Marx. See further P. Haubtmann, *Marx et Proudhon*, Paris, 1947, pp. 48–97, and W. Pickles, "Marx and Proudhon" in *Politica*, Vol. 3, no. 13, pp. 236–60, London, September, 1938, which also has a valuable account of Proudhon's style of argument.

from meaning what is expressed in the pure theory of association. We must live, that is to say, buy bread, fuel, meat, and we must pay our rent. And good heavens! a man who sells ideas about society is no less meritorious than one who sells a sermon. I know nothing about Grün's having made himself out to be my tutor. Tutor in what? I am only concerned with political economy, a subject about which he knows practically nothing. I regard literature as a plaything for little girls, and as for my philosophy, I know enough about it to be able to make light of it on occasion. Grün revealed nothing at all to me, and if he claims to have done so, he has been presumptuous and I am sure he regrets it.

But what I do know, and value more than I condemn a slight attack of vanity, is that it is to M. Grün and also to his friend Ewerbeck that I owe my knowledge of your writings, my dear M. Marx, and those of M. Engels, as well as of Feuerbach's very important work. At my request these gentlemen have been good enough to make several analyses for me in French (for unfortunately I am quite unable to read German) of the most important socialist publications. And it is at their entreaty that I have to make some mention (as I would have done of my own accord in any case) in my next work of the works of Messrs. Marx, Engels, Feuerbach, etc. ... Lastly, Grün and Ewerbeck are working to keep alive the sacred flame among the German colony in Paris, and the respect that the workers who consult them have for these gentlemen seems to me to be a sure guarantee of the honesty of their intentions.

It would give me much pleasure, my dear M. Marx, to see you reverse a judgment resulting from momentary irritation, for you were in an angry frame of mind when you wrote to me. Grün has told me of his wish to translate my present book. I realize that this translation more than any other would be of help to him. I would therefore be grateful, not on my own account but on his, if you and your friends would aid him on this occasion by helping to sell a work that, with your help, would doubtless benefit him more than myself.

If you would assure me of your assistance, my dear M. Marx, I will send my proofs to M. Grün immediately. I think that notwithstanding your personal grievances, on which I do not intend to pass judgment, this course of action would be a credit to all parties.

Your humble servant.

Kindest regards to your friends Messrs. Engels and Gigot.

Confessions pp. 432–37

XI   THE 1848 REVOLUTION AND THE SECOND EMPIRE

The February Revolution

I can hear the workers shouting: "Long live the Republic! Down with hypocrisy!" Poor souls! They are in the grips of *hypocrisy*. The very people who are going to become rulers are its unwitting agents and the first to be taken in. Intrigue is rife and gossip wins the day. Drunk on historical novels, we have given a repeat performance of the 10th of August and the 29th of July.[51] Without noticing it, we have all become characters from some farce.

All the events which have taken place before my own eyes, and in which I participated without much faith, are thoroughly artificial and give no signs of primitive spontaneity. Would that I were mistaken! But today I have become convinced of our decadence. Our only hope can

[51] The Revolution of August 10, 1792, marked the end of Louis XVI's rule; the Revolution of July 29–30, 1830, that of Charles X.

be that some serious, powerful ideas—taken from somewhere other than Robespierre's speeches—will revitalize our minds and give strength to our characters.

It may be that I am not in a good position to judge. My body is physically among the people, but my mind is elsewhere. My thinking has led me to the point where I have almost nothing in common with my contemporaries by way of ideas, and I would rather believe that my point of view is wrong than accuse them of madness . . . .

(February 25, 1848)   C 2, p. 284

To Maurice

I in no way helped to instigate the February Revolution. What I wanted was slow, measured, rational, philosophical progress. But events and human folly, particularly on the part of those mean, middle-of-the-road bourgeois, of which you are one, decided otherwise. I vowed to myself that I would do all that lay in my power to prevent the fruits of the February Revolution from being lost. I told myself that, as a penalty for our foolishness, we had to accomplish in one year what would normally take a century.

I believe that the aims I have set myself will be realized. You can repeat as often as you like that France does not want the Reds.[52] What is the use of that? As if it were a question of what France *wants;* as if we were not all at the moment governed by NECESSITY.

Now it was essential to bring this necessity to light, and the socialist, democratic agitation has done this very well. The old world is falling apart, and I defy you, in spite of all your philosophy and experience, to put it together again. Whether it likes it or not, the whole of Europe, in France's wake, has embarked upon a social

[52] Cf. footnote 57 below, p. 165.

revolution that I know may well sweep away both its originators and its opponents. Nobody has the power to stop it. The social body has swallowed the poison and, however much the sick man may writhe, his body in the end must be completely transformed and the old one be ignominiously cast away.

(March 3, 1849)   *C* 2, p. 363–64

To F***

Any revolution from above is inevitably, and I will explain the reason for this later, revolution which takes place through a prince's good pleasure, a minister's whim, the gropings of an assembly or the violence of a club. It is revolution by dictatorship and despotism . . . .

Revolution that is instigated by the masses is based on the concerted action of the citizens, the experience of the workers, and the increase and spreading of enlightenment. It is revolution based on liberty . . . .

It is a contradiction in terms to say that a government can be revolutionary, for the simple reason that it is the government. Only society, that is, the masses inspired with intelligence, can revolutionize itself, because only society can make rational use of its own spontaneous energy, can analyze and explain the mystery of its destiny and origins, can change its faith and its philosophy—and finally because only society is capable of struggling against its creator and of producing its own fruit. Governments are God's scourges set up to *discipline* the world. How then can you expect them to destroy themselves, engender liberty and start revolutions?

This is an impossibility. All revolutions, since the first king was crowned down to the Declaration of the Rights of Man, have been brought about spontaneously by the people. If there have been times when governments have followed the people's lead, this has been because they were forced to do so. Nearly always governments have prevented, repressed and struck at revolution. They have never, of their own accord, revolutionized anything. Their role is not to aid progress but to hold it back. Even if, which is unthinkable, they understood the science of revolution or social science, they could not put it into practice. They would not have the right to do so.

(1849)   *Confessions* pp. 81–82

The fact is that the revolution in the nineteenth century was not conceived within the bosom of any particular sect. It is not the consequence of any particular speculative principle or the consecration of any particular class or corporate interest. Revolution is the inevitable synthesis of all previous movements in philosophy, politics, social economics, etc. It exists, like the elements which compose it, of itself. It comes, in fact, neither *from above* nor *from below*. It is the result of principles being worn out, of the opposition of ideas, of conflicting interests, political contradictions, antagonistic prejudices, in short, of everything that seems best suited to convey the idea of moral and intellectual chaos . . . .

Yes, a God is watching over the new revolution. But what God? Is it the heroism of the people, the devotion of the bourgeoisie, the proverbial *furia francese*, the sudden realization of power? No. The power that presides over our destinies uses much simpler methods. You will witness neither conversions nor miracles. Politics fail and human wisdom is vain. What guarantees the triumph of the revolutionary cause is what one might consider as the most likely cause of its failure, namely the moderation that is characteristic of the French nation, its distinctive desire for preserving the golden mean, its inherent need for stability, and the horror it has always shown for disorders!

(1849)   *Confessions* p. 344

F*

Toast to the Revolution[53]

Citizens,

When our friends of the Democratic Republic, who are disturbed by our ideas and our tendencies, protest at our having qualified the word *democrat* by *socialist,* what do they reproach us for? They are reproaching us for not being revolutionaries.

Let us therefore decide whether it is we or they who are in the revolutionary tradition; whether it is we or they who are truly revolutionary in practice.

And when our bourgeois opponents, who are fearful for their privileges, pour down calumny and abuse upon us, what is the pretext for their accusations? It is that we want to pull down and destroy everything, property, the family, civilization.

Let us therefore also decide whether it is we or our opponents who better deserve the name conservative.

Revolutions are the successive manifestations of JUSTICE operating in human life. This is why the starting point of each revolution lies in a previous revolution.

Thus to speak of revolution is necessarily to speak of *progress* and thereby of *conservation.* So it follows that in history there is permanent revolution and that, strictly speaking, there have not been several revolutions, but only one and the same permanent revolution.

Confessions pp. 398–99

[53] This is an extract from Proudhon's speech at the Banquet of the Republic held in Montmartre on October 15, 1848, presided over by Lamennais and published in Proudhon's own paper, *Le Peuple,* on October 17. Here Proudhon relates his own socialist republicanism to the French Revolutionary tradition, in contrast to the Jacobin Republicanism of his opponents in the Republican party, i.e., Ledru-Rollin and the other "friends of the Democratic Republic."

The Idea of Revolution

A revolution is a force against which no other force, be it human or divine, can prevail. By its nature it gains strength and grows through the very opposition it encounters. A revolution may be directed, restrained or retarded . . . . The wisest course in politics is to give way to it inch by inch so that instead of proceeding by leaps and bounds, humanity's eternal evolution may proceed imperceptibly and without causing an upheaval. One cannot stem the tide of revolution, deceive it, distort it, and still less can one defeat it. The more you repress it, the more you are tightening its spring, and the more irresistible you are making its action; so much so that for an idea to be successful it is quite immaterial whether it be persecuted, harassed or suppressed when it first appears, or whether it develops and spreads without hindrance. Like Nemesis of old, whom neither entreaty nor threats could move, revolution advances with inevitable and menacing tread on the flowers strewn before it by its devotees, through the blood of its defenders and over the corpses of its enemies . . . .

In the first instance revolutions claim to be voicing the people's grievances, and indicting a corrupt state of affairs in which the poor are always the first to suffer. It is not in the nature of the masses to revolt, except against what harms them physically or morally. Are these grounds for repression, vengeance or persecution? What folly! Any government whose policy is to evade the aspirations of the masses and reject their grievances condemns itself out of its own mouth. It is like the evildoer who tries to overcome his remorse by committing further crimes. At each outrage the pangs of conscience become more terrible until finally the criminal's reason gives way and delivers him up to the executioner.

There is, as I have said, only one way of averting the dangers of revolution. It is by making revolution legitimate. The people suffer and are discontented with their lot. They are like men groaning in sickness, or children crying in their cradles. Anticipate their wants, listen to their grievances, discover the causes, the consequences, and exaggerate these if need be. Then set about healing the patient immediately and constantly. In these conditions revolution will take place without causing disruption, as part of the natural and proper development of the old order. Nobody will notice it or suspect that it is taking place. The grateful people will look upon you as their benefactor, their representative, their leader. This was how, in 1789, Louis XVI was greeted by the National Assembly and the people as the *Restorer of Public Liberty*. At his hour of glory Louis XVI, who was more powerful than his forebear Louis XIV, could have secured his house for centuries. He could have used the Revolution as a means of government, but the fool saw it only as an infringement of his rights. He carried this inconceivable blindness with him to the scaffold.

Alas, it seems that peaceful revolution is too ideal a thing for man, with his bellicose nature, to accept. Events seldom follow the most natural and least destructive course, although there is ample opportunity for them to do so. Just as the origins of revolution lie in the urgency of people's needs, so those of the forces of reaction are to be found in the authority of custom. The *status quo* always wants to prescribe against poverty, and this is why reaction initially gains the ascendancy that the revolution comes to enjoy in the end. As a result of this advance in opposite directions, in which one man's gain invariably means another man's loss, a violent struggle is much to be feared.

Two things militate against gradual revolution: vested interests and the pride of the government.

Through a determinism which will become plain later,

these two things always act in conjunction with each other in such a way that wealth and power, together with tradition, are ranged on one side, and poverty, disorder and the unknown on the other. The satisfied party does not wish to make any concessions, the injured party can no longer accept his position, and thus conflict gradually becomes inevitable.

(1851)   *Revn.* pp. 101–3

A revolution is, in the moral sphere, an act of sovereign justice that results from the force of circumstances. Consequently it is its own justification and it is a crime for a statesman to resist it . . . .

The causes of revolution are not so much the passing ills felt by society as the persistence of these ills, which tends to eliminate and cancel out the good.

Thus the trial instigated by a revolution, and the verdict that is later delivered, is less concerned with facts than with *intentions*, as if society were little troubled about *principles* and were chiefly guided by objectives ...

Generally speaking, good and evil, pleasure and pain, are inextricably mingled in the destiny of mankind. However, although the pendulum constantly swings back and forth between the two, good seems to triumph over evil, and all in all, in our judgment, there is marked progress toward the better.

The will of the masses is based on this assumption. Being neither optimistic nor pessimistic, the people do not accept the existence of any kind of absolute.

Since they believe that after all reforms there still remain some abuses to be got rid of, or some form of corruption to be fought against, they content themselves with seeking what is better or less bad, and work toward their own salvation through labor, study and morals. Their code of conduct therefore consists of a TENDENCY TOWARD

WELL-BEING AND VIRTUE, and they revolt only if there is a *tendency toward poverty and corruption . . . .*

The question that we started with as the subject of this study, namely, *"can revolution in the nineteenth century be justified?"* therefore becomes the question *"in what direction is society moving today?" . . . .*

Let us go back to the starting point of this society, to the year 1789.

In 1789 the Revolution had both to destroy and to build. It had to abolish the *ancien régime* and it had to produce a new system whose scheme and features had to be different in every way from those of the old order. According to the revolutionary law, "every negation in Society implies a subsequent and contradictory affirmation."

The Revolution accomplished only the first of these two things, and even that was with great difficulty; the second was completely forgotten. This is the reason why France has not had a viable social system for the last sixty years.

Thus when the feudal regime was abolished on the night of August 4,[54] and the principle of liberty and civil equality was proclaimed, society should thereafter have been organized in terms of labor and not in terms of politics and war. For what, in fact, was the feudal organization? It was a wholly military organization. And what is labor? It is the very opposite of combat. By abolishing feudalism man was sentencing himself to perpetual peace, not only with other countries, but also at home. By this one act, the whole of the old political structure based on relations between States and all the structures insuring the balance of power in Europe were abrogated. The equality and independence which the Revolution prom-

---

[54] 1789, the feverish night session of the Constituent Assembly when the nobility, in an attempt to appease the peasantry, renounced many of their feudal privileges.

ised would reign between citizens should also have been
made to prevail between nation and nation, province and
province, city and city.

Therefore what had to be organized after August 4 was
not government, since to organize a government would
simply have been to re-establish the old structures; rather,
it was the national economy and balance of interests. Since
under the new law birth was no longer a determining
factor in the condition of the citizen, and labor alone, on
which property itself depended, was all that counted, and
since in foreign affairs, the relations between nations
had to be reforged in the light of these principles (given
that civil law, public law and the rights of individuals are
equal and identical), it was clear that the task facing the
Revolution when it had abolished the feudal or military
regime in France and in Europe was to set up everywhere
instead an egalitarian industrial regime. The progress in
agriculture that was marked immediately after the national
wealth had been shared out, the industrial progress of
the nation after the fall of the Empire, and the increasing
interest, after 1830, in economic questions that was noticeable in all countries, have proved that political economy is indeed the sphere in which the Revolution ought
to concentrate its efforts . . . .

To be brief, my view, however unedifying it may be, is
that the Revolutionaries failed to fulfill their own mission
from the moment they took the Bastille, just as they failed
immediately after the February Revolution [of 1848], and
for the same reasons. They had no notion of economics,
they believed in government, and they mistrusted the
proletariat. In 1793 the necessity of resisting invasion demanded an enormous concentration of forces, thus inno-
vation was out of the question. The principle of centralization that was widely applied by the Committee of Public
Safety became a dogma for the Jacobins, who handed it
down to the Empire and the governments that succeeded

it. Such is the unhappy tradition that in 1848 was responsible for the retrograde course of the Provisional Government and that still at present is accepted as definitive and constitutes the staple food of the Republican party.

(1851)   *Revn.* pp. 123–27

We must find a way out of that vicious circle. We must cast aside the political ideal and the old notion of distributive justice, and adopt that of commutative justice, which in the natural course of events and of the law must take its place. You are willfully blind, you who seek in the clouds for what you have within your grasp. Reread your writers, look about you, analyze your own tenets, and you will discover the solution has been with us down the centuries from time immemorial, though neither you nor your leaders have ever deigned to notice.

(1851)   *Revn.* p. 186

The Imperial Regime

I believe that the penalty we paid on December 2[55], however deplorable, was the strictly logical consequence of the ideas that predominated in France between February and December '51. All the parties were conspiring, plotting a *coup d'état*. All were calling for dictatorship. Success went to the most daring or to the most diligent, whichever you prefer.

What followed is exactly, or almost exactly the same as what would have happened if instead of L.B.[56] we

[55] 1851, the date of Napoleon III's *coup d'état*.
[56] Louis Bonaparte, i.e. Napoleon III.

had had the Reds, the Whites or the Blues.[57] The performance would have been the same but the actors would have been different. Of course December 2 has stained our virtue, but it has done credit to our logic. The French people behaved point for point in accordance with the maxims of the so-called *revolutionary* party, which was, as a matter of fact, in complete agreement with the absolutists.

At present it seems to me that L.B. is making a singular mistake as to the meaning of his victory, and as to his true interests. In order to retain the votes of honest citizens, his entourage, his courtesans (let us call them his exploiters) have hastened to give a conservative tone to his usurpation of power, so that he is placed in a perpetually false position. For L.B.'s only followers are the ignorant masses, precisely those people for whom there ought to be social reforms, and yet he throws himself in with the legitimists, the Orleanists, the priestly rabble—all the factions the people have learned to hate, whom they hate all the more the more they admire the Emperor, and who ought to be eliminated. As a result of this we have a policy based on nepotism and permanent eclecticism that wavers between Caesarism and democracy, between revolution and counterrevolution, etc. At this very moment the legitimists are preparing for L.B.'s succession. Nobody believes that he is here to stay or that he will last for long. As for the Republicans, they are dying of hunger and poverty abroad. Meanwhile, the Revolutionary ideal continues to make progress. The President has postulated it in his few attempts at reform, and translated it into real terms. It exists and has already started to be put into effect. Given all these things, it seems to me quite legitimate to expect further *snags* and *flukes*, and it is with

[57] "The Reds" was the term for the socialist revolutionaries; white was the monarchist color, blue that of the moderate Republicans.

these in mind that I am getting as big a start as I can and preparing to give my worthy contemporaries a further lesson.[58]

(March 21, 1852)   *C* 4, p. 260

To Laurent

What the prophets of social transformation did not themselves foresee is that INDUSTRIAL FEUDALISM[59] is no more solidly established than INDUSTRIAL ANARCHY had been. This is only another crisis that must pass like the first:

Sic erat instabilis tellus, innabilis unda.[60]

Anarchy and feudalism, history shows, both result from a lack of equilibrium, from antagonism and from social warfare. Given people's state of mind at present, there seems to be no remedy for this except in a more powerful concentration of a third term in the series, which without any ill intent we will call INDUSTRIAL EMPIRE . . . .

INDUSTRIAL EMPIRE is in fact the very principle of anarchy, the famous *laissez faire laissez passer* taken to the extreme, a *reductio ad absurdum* of classical, official political economy. In a word, it is a contradiction.

(1857)   *Manual* p. viii

[58] Which he did in his *The Social Revolution as exemplified by the coup d'état of December 2*, where he suggested Napoleon III could usher in a new age of social reform—a view Proudhon quickly abandoned. To get the book past the censor, Proudhon had to appeal to the Emperor himself; together with the substance of his argument this hardly improved Proudhon's reputation among European democrats and revolutionaries.

[59] An extension of the term "financial feudalism" used by Lamartine and then by Toussenel in *The Jews, Kings of the Epoch: the Financial Feudalism* (cf. note 100 below, p. 227).

[60] "Though there was both land and sea, no one could tread that land, or swim that sea": from Ovid's description of the time before the creation of Heaven and Earth in *Metamorphoses,* I. 16.

INDUSTRIAL DEMOCRACY must, in accordance with the law of historical antinomies, succeed *Industrial Feudalism.* This follows from the opposition of the terms just as day follows night.

But what agent will bring about this revolution?

Once again history provides the answer. Between the old feudal order and the final liquidation we will therefore have an economic concentration, or, to be plain, an *Industrial Empire.*

(1857)   *Manual* p. 449

XII THE WORKING CLASSES AND THE BOURGEOISIE

Class Contradictions in the State

From the moment that the State is constituted the contradictions implicit in the very concept of it are the seeds of its own destruction . . . .

Since war and inequality of fortune have always been the people's lot, society becomes divided naturally into a number of different classes: warriors or nobles, priests, landowners, merchants, seafarers, industrial workers and peasants. Royalty, where it exists, forms its own exclusive caste above all others, namely dynasty.

The struggle among the classes, their conflicting interests and the way in which these interests unite, determines the political system and consequently the type of government with its innumerable varieties and its even more innumerable variations. But little by little all classes are reduced to two: the upper, that is, an aristocracy, bourgeoisie or patriciate, and the lower, that is, the common people or proletariat. Wavering between the two is royalty, which is the organ of power and expression of authority. If the aristocracy unites with royalty, the resulting government will be a mild form of monarchy, that known as constitutional. If it is the people who join forces with authority, the government will be an Empire or autocratic democracy.

(1863)   *Fed.* pp. 294, 296

However logically sound a federal constitution may be, and whatever guarantees it offers in practice, it will not be a viable system until all disruptive forces in the public economy have been eliminated. In other words, political law must be founded on economic law. If the production and distribution of wealth is left to chance, if the federal system merely serves to protect the anarchy of commercial capitalism, and if as a result of this pseudo-anarchy society is divided into two classes, on the one hand the property-owning capitalist industrialists and on the other the wage-earning proletariat, i.e. the rich and the poor, the political structure will always be unstable. The working class, that is, the poorest and most numerous class,[61] will finally see that it was merely a trick, and they will unite against the bourgeoisie, who in turn will unite against the workers. If the people are the stronger the confederation will degenerate into a centralized democracy, and if the bourgeoisie gain the upper hand, it will degenerate into constitutional monarchy.

As I said in a previous chapter, it is against the eventuality of social war that strong governments have been set up. These are much admired by political writers who consider that the frail structures of a confederation are

[61] Proudhon is here using Saint-Simon's phrase: *"la classe la plus nombreuse et la plus pauvre."*

not strong enough to defend a government against the attack of the masses, that is to say, to defend government interests against the rights of the nation. For let me repeat, and let there be no mistake about it, all governments, citadels and armies are set up and organized as much against attack from the inside as from the outside. If it is the State's mission to reign as absolute monarch in society, and if it is the people's destiny to serve as the means by which it carries out its plans, then indeed it must be confessed that the federal system cannot bear comparison with the system of centralized government.

But everything indicates that times have changed, and that the natural consequence of the revolution in ideas must be a revolution of interests. The twentieth century will usher in the age of federations, or else humanity will fall back into purgatory for another thousand years. The real problem to be solved is not a political one, it is an economic one.

(1863)   *Fed.* p. 354

The federal system very adequately satisfies both democratic ideals and bourgeois conservatism, two things that cannot in any other circumstances be reconciled. How does it do this? It does it through the politico-economic guarantees that are the most valuable features of federalism. When France has returned to its natural state—based on the law of medium-sized property, honest mediocrity and equality, with as far as possible a leveling-out of fortunes, a France that has recaptured its spirit and its own way of life, and is composed of a cluster of sovereignties that are mutually guaranteed—she will have nothing to fear from the onslaught of communism nor from the incursions of monarchy. The masses, who will from then on be powerless to repress public liberty, will be equally powerless to seize or confiscate property. Better still, they will become the strongest barrier against the feudalization of land and capital that inevitably takes place in a centralized state. While the town dweller values property only for the revenue it provides, the peasant who cultivates it values it for its own sake, which is why property is never better guaranteed than when, by a permanent, well-regulated division, it approaches equality and federation. No more bourgeoisie, no more democracy; let us have, as we demanded in 1848, nothing but citizens. Is this not what the Revolution really means? Where would you find the fulfillment of this ideal if not in Federalism?

(1863)   *Fed.* p. 549

Proudhon's election address at Doubs in 1848

I must insist upon my opposition to the Provisional Government [of the 1848 Revolution] and I will keep it up until I see a change of system.

Dear fellow countrymen, through the studies of economics I have pursued during the last ten years, through daily experience at workbench and counter, through what is taking place before my very eyes, and through the news I receive daily from the provinces, I have become more and more convinced of the truth of one thing. This is that, in a situation in which the social problem must be solved urgently and without delay, the only hope for the working class, for the bourgeoisie, for everyone, in fact, lies in all parties being willing to solve the problem jointly.

C 2, p. 300

The Bourgeoisie

The Gods have departed, the kings are withdrawing, privilege is disappearing, everyone counts himself one of the workers. While the taste for comfort and elegance is tearing the masses away from *sans-culottism,* the aristocracy, alarmed by the smallness of their numbers, seeks its salvation within the ranks of the petite-bourgeoisie. France, whose true nature is becoming more and more marked, gave the incentive, and the Revolution is making its triumphant appearance, embodied in the middle class.

(1851 Postscript)   *Confessions* p. 373

Class Consciousness

The 1863 elections were the first time that the Republican opposition candidates got more votes than the Imperial Government's candidates in the Paris region. Proudhon interpreted this as showing that the industrial working class had abandoned the Empire. Proudhon had taken part in a campaign favoring abstention to protest the regime's restriction of political and municipal liberties. During this election three working-class candidates were proposed, though in the end only two stood, receiving 343 votes between them. In 1864 further elections were held, and this time Henri Tolain stood as the sole working-class candidate, receiving 424 votes. In support of his candidacy a committee of working-class democrats published a *Manifesto of the Sixty,* which greatly impressed Proudhon and led him to set down his views of working-class political action (or rather, economic action) in *On the Political Capacity of the Working Classes* (cf. above Section III on Mutualism). Tolain was one of the first members of the French section of the First International, founded in 1864. At the Congresses of the International, he defended Proudhon's views on the place of women in society and opposed the Marxist view on the issue of the working class and direct political action.--S.E.

The peasants' cause is the same as that of the industrial workers. The socialist in the city has his counterpart in the Marianne[62] of the fields. They have the same opponents. Until 1863 the two large laboring classes, the peasants and industrial workers, had both voted for the Emperor without making any agreement to do so, but in 1863 and 1864, while the peasants remained loyal to the Imperial standard, the industrial workers, for no very good reason, went over to the bourgeoisie. By this I am not implying that they would have done better to emulate their brothers in the fields. I simply mean that it would have been more worthy if they had set the example by declaring that in future they intended to be independent. It is up to the industrial democrats in Paris and the large towns who have taken the lead to discover what they have in common with the peasant democrats, not to make it appear to freemen that they support the fief system.

(1865)   *Pol. Cap.* p. 69

Political capacity or capability in any subject, be it individual, corporation, or collective body, depends upon the existence of three basic conditions:

1. The subject must be *conscious* of himself, his dignity, his worth, his place in society, the role he plays, the functions to which he may rightfully aspire and the interests he represents or embodies.

2. As a result of this consciousness of himself and all his possibilities, the said subject must affirm his *idea;* that is to say, he must be able to present himself through his intelligence, put into words and give a rational account of the principles and consequences of the law of his being.

3. When he has made this idea an article of faith, he must always be able to draw *practical* conclusions from

---

[62] Name given to the French Republic since the Revolution.

it, which will vary according to the demands of circumstances.

It should be noted that there can be no question of more or less. Some men feel things more keenly than others. Their consciousness of themselves is exalted to a greater or lesser extent. They understand the idea and expound it with a greater or lesser amount of skill and energy, or they have a gift for practical application that often outstrips that of the most intelligent minds. Although these differences of intensity of consciousness, of the idea and its application constitute *degrees* of capacity, they do not create the capacity itself . . . .

Being politically capable does not mean having a particular aptitude for the affairs of State or for performing a particular public function. It does not mean having a certain burning zeal for civic concerns. These things, I repeat, are a question of talent and specialization, and are not the ground for what I mean here by political capacity in the citizen, who is often silent, modest and holds no public office. Having political capacity means being *conscious* of oneself as a member of a collectivity. It means affirming the resulting *idea* and working toward its *realization*. Any person who fulfills these three conditions is politically capable. For example, we all feel ourselves to be FRENCHMEN, and as such we believe in a constitution, and we believe that our country has a mission. In the light of these things, through our wishes and our votes, we give preference to the policies that seem best to interpret our feelings and correspond to our opinions. The spirit of patriotism may be more or less ardent in each of us, but its nature is the same and its absence an abnormality. Thus in three words, we have *consciousness*, we have an *idea*, and we pursue its *realization*.

In dealing with the question of the political capacity of the working class, or of the bourgeoisie, or, as formerly, of the nobility, we must consider the following points: (a) whether the working class, in its relations with society and with the State, has acquired consciousness of itself; whether as a collective, moral, free being, it is distinct from the bourgeoisie; (b) whether it has its own idea, that is to say, whether it has created a notion of its own constitution; whether it knows the laws, conditions and formulae of its existence; whether it foresees its destiny or end; whether it understands its relations with the State, the nation and the universal order; and finally, (c) whether the working class is in a position to draw from this idea its own practical conclusions for the organizing of society, and whether, in the event of coming to power as the result of the downfall or retreat of the bourgeoisie, it would be able to create and develop a new political order.

This is political capacity. We are, of course, speaking of the *real*, collective capacity which is a fact of nature and society and results from the activity of the human spirit. Apart from inequalities of talent and consciousness, it is found in all individuals and cannot become the particular privilege of any one person. It is present in all religious communities, sects, corporations, castes, parties, States, nationalities, etc. It is a capacity which the legislator is ill-equipped to create, but which he is obliged to seek and which, in any event, he believes to exist.

It is in the light of this definition of political capacity that I reply in connection with the working classes, disregarding their shortcomings and sheep-like behavior, still a sad daily spectacle, in the following way:

On the first point: yes, the working classes have acquired consciousness of themselves and we can fix 1848 as the time of this awakening.

On the second point: yes, the working classes do have an idea that corresponds to their consciousness of themselves, and this idea is in direct contrast to that of the bourgeoisie. Yet one may say that this idea has not so far been fully revealed to them, that they have not followed up all its consequences and have not yet found the formula for it.

On the third point, relating to the political conclusions that may be drawn from the idea: no, the working classes, although they are sure of themselves and are already semi-enlightened about the principle of their new faith, have not yet managed to deduce from it any standard practice or appropriate policy. In this respect, witness the fact that they voted with the bourgeoisie, and witness also their numerous political prejudices.

Let us say, in words that smack less of the classroom, that the working classes are only just being born into political life. If, through the initiative they are beginning to take, and by sheer weight of numbers, they have been able to displace the center of gravity within the political order and shake up the social economy, they have not yet, on the other hand, been able to dominate, because of the intellectual chaos from which they suffer, and particularly because of the capricious treatment they have received at the hands of a bourgeoisie *in extremis*. The working classes have even retarded their emancipation and to some extent compromised their future.

(1865)   *Pol. Cap.* pp. 89–92

In spite of their devotion to the ideas of '89, the Opposition political writers have not realized that what has created the new distinction between the bourgeoisie and the working class or proletariat—a distinction that was quite unknown in feudal times, and this just at the moment when the old categories of Nobility, Clergy and Third Estate are disappearing—is precisely the rights established in '89. They have not realized that before '89 the worker lived in the guild, just as women, children and servants live in the family; prior to this, it would not have been acceptable to admit the existence of a class of workers as opposed to a class of entrepreneurs, since the former were supposed to be a part of the latter. Since '89 the body of guilds has been broken, although the means and conditions of worker and master have not been equalized. Nothing was done; no plans were made for the distribution of capital, for the organizing of industry, or for the rights of workers. As a result, the distinction between the class of employers, owners of the means of production, capitalists and large property owners, and that of simple wage-earners has grown up of its own accord . . . .

Our entire political system, our public economy, our industrial organization, contemporary history, and particularly our literature are all grounded in this inevitable distinction, and it would be a sign of bad faith and foolish hypocrisy to deny it.

(1865)   *Pol. Cap.* pp. 94, 96

Whether the bourgeoisie knows it or not, its role is at an end; it cannot escape and it cannot be reborn. But let it die a peaceful death. The rise to power of the common people does not mean that they will eliminate it, in the sense that the people will gain political domination over the bourgeoisie and then take over its privileges, property and rights, while the bourgeoisie will take the place of the people as wage-earners. The present, firmly established distinction between the two classes of workers and bourgeoisie is simply an accident of revolution. Each must absorb the other into a greater consciousness. The day when the common people constitute the majority, when they have seized power and have instituted economic and social reform in accord with the aspirations of the new law and science, will be the day when they both fuse forever. It is in the light of these new circumstances that the people, who for so long have lived only in hostility, must in future define themselves, manifest their independence and establish their political existence.

(1865)   *Pol. Cap.* p. 101

Modern socialism was not founded as a sect or church; it has seen a number of different schools. The working classes have not bound themselves to any one master. Cabet, the Icarian dictator, learned this the hard way at Nauvoo.[63] They have followed their own inspiration, and it is unlikely that they will at any time give up their own independence of action. This is the guarantee of their success.

A social revolution, such as that of '89, which working-class democracy is continuing under our eyes, is a spontaneous transformation that takes place throughout the body politic. It is the substitution of one system for another, a new organism replacing one that is outworn. But this change does not take place in a matter of minutes, as a man changes his dress or cockade. It does not happen at the command of one man who has his own pre-established theory, or at the dictate of some prophet. A truly organic revolution is a product of universal life, and although it may have its emissaries and executives it is not really the work of any single person. It is an idea that is at first very rudimentary and that germinates like a seed; an idea that is at first in no way remarkable since it is based on popular wisdom, but one that, like the seed buried in the earth or the embryo in the egg, suddenly grows in a most unexpected fashion and fills the world with its institutions

[63] Cabet called his socialist utopia Icaria. A group of his followers sailed to the United States to found an Icarian colony. Cabet later joined them in 1851 at Nauvoo in Illinois. At first the colony prospered, but disagreements arose and Cabet, finding his authority resented, had to leave, taking with him two hundred of his followers. Cabet died soon after his return to France.

. . . . It has been the same with the working-class idea in the nineteenth century . . . .

The people had acquired consciousness of themselves and were aware of themselves. The disturbance [of the Revolution of 1789] that had arisen around them and because of them had awakened their intelligence. A bourgeois revolution had just conferred political rights on them. Summonsed, so to speak, to make their thoughts clear without the aid of interpreters, they followed the logic of their situation. First, setting themselves up as henceforth distinct from the bourgeoisie, the people tried to turn bourgeois maxims back upon the bourgeoisie. They imitated them; then, learning from their lack of success and abandoning their first hypothesis, they sought salvation in an original idea.

(1865)   *Pol. Cap.* pp. 110–12

Under the impulse of an energetic consciousness, and thanks to the power of a correct idea, the People reveal themselves to the world with the strength and vivacity of an organic body, claiming their place in the councils of nations and offering the middle classes an alliance that they will shortly be only too pleased to secure; whereas we can see that the haute-bourgeoisie, which has trundled along from one political catastrophe to another and has reached the lowest possible degree of intellectual and moral vacuity, is dissolving into a mass whose only remaining human feature is egoism. They look for saviors when there is no salvation left for them, they display a cynical indifference to all policies, and rather than accept inevitable change, call down upon the nation and upon themselves the waters of a second Flood, relentlessly rejecting those things which they themselves greeted in 1789: Law, Science, Progress, or, in a word, Justice.

(1865)   *Pol. Cap.* p. 231

The army of liberty and progress will always be formed by the people, by virtue of their subjection and poverty. Labor is republican by nature and would be contradictory if it were otherwise. But because of their ignorance, the primitive nature of their instincts, the urgency of their needs and the impatience of their desires, the people incline toward summary forms of authority. They do not want legal guarantees, for they know nothing about these and do not understand their importance, nor do they want a well-organized, proper balance of forces, which they would not know how to use. What they want is a leader whose word they can trust, whose intentions they are familiar with and who devotes himself to their cause. They invest this leader with unlimited authority, with power none can withstand. The people, who identify the right with the useful simply because they are the people, do not bother about formalities; they attach no importance to conditions imposed on the holders of power. They are quick to suspect and to slander, but are incapable of methodical discussion. Their only real belief is in the human will, their only hope lies in man and they trust only what he has created, *in principibus, in filiis hominum;*[64] they expect nothing from principles, which alone can save them, and they have no faith in any system of ideas.

(1863)   *Fed.* p. 301

It is now for the working class to understand their destiny and to decide accordingly on their course of action. All the economic reforms that I put forward in 1848 as necessary to the abolition of the proletariat, and which were interpreted by some as leading toward communism, lead in fact to the more equal distribution of property

[64] "In the leaders and in the sons of man."

and the firm establishment of this institution. Let us assume for the sake of argument that the liquid and fixed capital of France is 120,000 milliards of francs and the number of families 10,000,000. The capital fortune per family will therefore be 12,000 francs. An estate worth 12,000 francs, if it is properly cultivated, is sufficient for one family to live on. Workers, this is where your future lies. This is where the future of our country lies. Put aside your ideas for sharing out all property, your plans for requisitioning, for progressive taxation, for price-fixing[65] for guilds and tariffs. Sharing, that is to say equal distribution, will take place of its own accord. It will take place more quickly and more effectively through labor, saving, the organization of credit and exchange, cheap services, equal taxation and the reduction of taxes to a "twentieth,"[66] through transfers of property, public education, and, above all things, through LIBERTY.

(1863–64)   *Property* p. 198

At present the working classes, rejecting bourgeois practices and turning eagerly toward a higher ideal, have conceived the notion of a guarantee that would liberate them both from the risk of the depreciation of prices and wages, and from the deadly remedy of workers' combinations [i.e. trade unions]. This guarantee consists partly of the principle of *association*, through which all over Europe they are preparing to organize legal workers' companies to compete with bourgeois concerns, and partly of the more general and more widespread principle of MUTUAL-

[65] A demand to return to the law of May 1793, fixing maximum prices, which was abolished in December 1794 following the fall of Robespierre.

[66] *Le vingtième* was first imposed in 1749; since then successive "twentieths" had raised this tax to well above its original five per cent.

ISM, through which working-class Democracy, putting a premium on solidarity and groups, is preparing the way for the political and economic reconstruction of society. It is the combined force of the two principles of association and mutualism—which we need not emphasize any further—that comprises the system of moral and material guarantees sought by humanity.

Thus I have the right to reproach the workers as follows and to ask why, when they support the notions of association and mutualism, they have abandoned their generous, revitalizing IDEA that must carry the common people well beyond the old forms of aristocratic and bourgeois society, and why they have suddenly revealed a certain hostility for their masters . . . .

While threatening to strike, some of them, indeed the majority, have demanded an increase in wages, others have demanded a reduction in working hours, and still others both at the same time. Surely they have always known that increased wages and reduced working hours can only lead to a general price increase. And surely they know that it is not a question of reducing or increasing prices and wages, but of making them equal. This is the first condition of wealth! . . . .

Once it has set foot on the slope toward arbitrariness, working-class Democracy will not be any more capable than despotism of checking its course. In certain trade associations employers are not allowed to take on any man if it is against the wishes of the members of the union. Similarly, employers cannot train apprentices, employ foreigners or apply new methods. We will soon have heard the last of association, mutualism and progress if the workers, following the example of the great monopolists, succeed in substituting extortion for free competition . . . .

If the laws of 1864 gave the workers the right to com-

G

bine against their employers,[67] it also gave the employers the same rights against them. Thus what we have is organized war between capital and labor. As things are at present, which do you [Proudhon is addressing the workers] think will win?

Let us imagine that an industrial establishment has a capital of three million and that it employs one thousand workers who one day go on strike. The employer rejects their demands . . . . After a month the workers have exhausted their funds and will have to resort to the pawnshop. The capitalist will have lost merely a twelfth of his interest and his capital will not have been touched. The match is clearly unequal . . . .

I must repeat that at the moment the middle class is being placed in an untenable position. I am not accusing anyone, neither the Government, who thought they were being liberal when they signed the Trade Treaty,[68] changed the laws on Combinations and started to study an even more disastrous law to free usury, nor high finance and the big companies, nor the large property owners . . . . But I am accusing the counterrevolutionary instincts of our age that are roused by the terror of socialism and the system of political centralization, counterbalanced by anarchical capitalism, which is incompatible with the liberties and guarantees of 1789 that were embodied in the middle class.

It seems to me that on all sides people are working fanatically to destroy and reduce to the level of wage-earners the middle class with whom, a year ago, the working-class democrats, somewhat better guided, wanted to identify themselves. Bankruptcy is daily causing large

[67] This piece of Imperial social legislation repealed the 1791 Anti-Combination Act thereby giving the workers a restricted right to strike.

[68] The Second Empire made a number of bilateral free trade treaties, the first being the Cobden-Chevalier Anglo-French Treaty of 1860.

gaps to appear in the ranks of the petite-bourgeoisie;
worse still, increasing privation, hand-to-mouth living and
hidden poverty are decimating them. The workers have
been aware only of their own distress; they do not suspect
the hardships suffered by the bourgeoisie. As a result of
the Anti-Combination laws, the workers have been placed
on the side of the capitalist aristocrats and against small-
scale industry, small business concerns and small property;
so in 1869 they will doubtless vote for the Government
candidates. This would be quite a logical thing to do.
Freedom to combine, free usury and free trade will deserve this token of their devotion at the expense of their
natural allies. But the workers had better give some
thought to the matter. It is not by contradictory acts of
this kind that they will place themselves at the head of
civilization and reform society. They will not convince
people of the strength of their Idea, nor will their political capacity reach the level of the science of economics,
if they basely give themselves up to the fantasies of the
counterrevolution.

(1865)   *Pol. Cap.* p. 395–99

XIII   THE QUESTION OF
NATIONALITIES

America

The spiritual poverty of the Americans becomes evident in their morals. What, in fact, is American society?
It is composed of commoners who have suddenly acquired wealth. Now fortune, far from civilizing men, most
often brings out their vulgarity. Talleyrand's comment
on the Americans is well known and I shall not repeat it

here, though there is undoubtedly some truth in it.[69]
The Americans present an exaggerated version of the
utilitarianism of the English, from whom they are largely
descended. English pride has become insolence, and English uncouthness, brutality. For the American, liberty is
defined as *the freedom to do anything that is disagreeable
to anyone else*. His motto is BE YOUR OWN DEFENDER. I
must say that if I should have to defend myself against a
vulgar individual I would far rather do so with the help
of a constable and, if need be, a jailer. This is the sort of
treatment that vulgarity deserves. People try to kill you,
rob you or assassinate you, and the motto is "be your own
defender!" Then there is lynch law, as I think it is called,
which operates in certain cases. On public outcry, the
culprit is arrested, sentenced and hanged, all in the space
of a few minutes. This was the way the people executed
justice during the February Revolution.[70] It is also the
justice of the court-martial. I would rather have that of
the jury.

(1861)   *War* p. 50

Have the Americans thought about the enormous problems of Economics that are being hatched by our century?
No, far from it. The Americans are perhaps more bent
on gain than any other nation, and they are less scrupulous
about bankruptcy. While one half of the nation, with
Bible in hand, cultivates slavery, the other is already creating a proletariat.

In short, the Americans are by tradition strangers to

[69] During his exile in America in the 1790s Talleyrand was
struck by the commercial spirit of the country; hence one of
the many anecdotes attributed to him is that he said to Barante,
"Don't speak to me about a country where I found no one
who wasn't ready to sell me his dog."

[70] That is, the 1848 French Revolution.

the moral, political and philosophical developments of the Old World. They are kept at a distance from it by their way of life and colonial concerns, and are aware only of their immense wealth and independence. These Americans are now catching all the vices by which we in Europe are being destroyed . . . .

Of course the workingman should receive some praise, and what have I done during the last twenty years other than to urge the masses among whom I was born to act as free men, following the example of the Americans? But I must add that the creation of wealth is, in law, only the foundation of the social structure. This is not what the nations live on. Above the realm of the useful there are other, more glorious realms: philosophy, science, art, law, morality. Human dignity can, if need be, do without wealth, as was proved by Pythagoras and his school. But what is a people if it has no philosophy, no art, no rational ideas of law and morality? It seems to me that the Americans neglect these things too much and this is the reason why, in spite of their dollars and their pride, they rank last among the civilized nations.

I could say a great deal more if I developed these thoughts further, but I would rather finish where I began. American society began at the point where European society will finish, namely, at liberty and democracy. This is the reason why it cannot understand what torments European society. The mission of American society is not to solve the problem of the future, but to produce some new and immensely important fact that will help to solve it, and to make sure that society can never again degenerate. If China and India, or Greece and Rome, had had, as we have now in America, the backing of another democracy, Greece and Rome would not have collapsed, and India and China would not be at the mercy of barbarians as they are at present. This is of enormous importance, and it will be eternally to the credit of the

American people that they have, so to speak, incarnated liberty in this way.

(December 30, 1860)   *C* 10, pp. 275–76

To Dulieu

Free Trade

The philosophical concept of free trade is very widespread today. It dominates not only the sphere of political economy, but tends, wherever it appears, to replace the principles of Morality, Law and even Art. This fundamentally false theory is the same thing as the well-known and much discredited theory of *Art for Art's sake, Love for Love's sake, Pleasure for Pleasure's sake, War for War's sake, Government for Government's sake,* and so on. All these formulae that disregard morality, science, law and the laws of logic, nature and the mind, can be reduced quite simply to: *Liberty for Liberty's sake.*

I say it is untrue that Liberty can by itself compensate for the laws of Consciousness and the principles of Science and Judgment. In other words, it is not true that Truth, Reason, Duty and Law, Love and Judgment are epitomized in the one word Liberty. Intelligence is not the same thing as Liberty; Love and Art are not the same thing as Liberty; Society and Justice, more particularly, are not the same thing as Liberty. And this is why if exchange, labor, credit and property are to be declared equitable, and more particularly, to be guaranteed, it is not enough for them to be free. I defend Liberty as much as any man; I desire it and claim it, but alone it does not satisfy me. In my economic relations with my fellow men I also require Truth, Mutualism and Law, just as I require judgment and good sense in Art, utility in Industry, and accuracy and method in Science . . . .

It is not true that a nation must abandon those indus-

tries which are the least productive and retain those
which produce the most. To do this would mean rejecting three quarters of man's labor. All production and
raw material originates in the soil. Now the soil differs
not only in its suitability; it also varies in its fertility. Since
the land has had to be divided among the people who
live on it, in the name of political and social solidarity the
more fortunate must somehow protect the less fortunate
by greater production and industry.

(1865)   *Pol. Cap.* pp. 354–55

In a republic the protection the State gives to the labor
and commerce of the country is a contract of guarantee
by virtue of which the citizens, other things being equal,
make mutual promises to give each other preference over
foreigners in all transactions. This preference is an integral
part of republican law and, I may observe in passing, it
is particularly true of the law of a federal republic. If
this were not the case what would be the use of being a
member of a republic? How could the citizen feel attached to an order that insultingly spurned the products
of his labor and industry in favor of those of the
foreigner? . . . .

I do not want to defend the institution of tariffs, since
it is no longer required by labor, but simply to justify its
aims . . . .

It was the aim and original idea of this institution to
create guarantees between producers and dealers. As a
direct result of this the workers' labor was guaranteed.

(1865)   *Pol. Cap.* pp. 349–50

When I call free trade a coalition, I do not of course
mean that those in power and the representatives of the
capitalist, commercial and industrial aristocracy are con-
spirators. No one in the upper or middle classes, the Gov-

ernment or even the schools has ever thought to the logical conclusion of free trade. The interested parties, as we have seen from speeches made in the Legislative Assembly, have never thought further than what has been called the *balance of trade*. What I want to denounce is the interrelation of economic factors which gives rise in the Government and aristocracy to a kind of logic or instinct that drives them toward their end with a certainty that looks like premeditation. But, I repeat, people's knowledge of economics is far from reaching such heights. If the upper classes are today characterized by any one feature, it is by the total absence of principles, or rather, total ignorance about the ideas that motivate them, and the policy of living from day to day.

(1865)　　*Pol. Cap.* p. 369

European Nationalism

It is one thing to pursue the regeneration of society, as I do daily, through philosophy, economics and law, that is, through the Revolution; it is quite another to try and decide how a statesman in a conservative government should act at any given moment . . . .

Yes, my situation is that I am a Catholic—or, if you prefer, clerical, because France, my country, is still Catholic, because the English are Anglican, the Prussians Protestant, the Swiss Calvinist, the Americans Unitarian and the Russians Orthodox; because while our missionaries are being martyred in Cochin China, English missionaries are selling Bibles and other articles of commerce . . . .

My patriotism is not in the least all-absorbing or exclusive. I will never put devotion to my country before the rights of man. If the French Government behaves unjustly to any people, I am deeply grieved and protest in every way that I can. If France is punished for the misdeeds of her leaders, I bow my head and say from the depth of my soul, *"Merito haec patimur."*[71] Brutus sacrificed his sons to his country, though this was probably not absolutely necessary. Were I forced to choose, I would be prepared to sacrifice my country to justice.

Having made this declaration in order to clear my conscience, I must now ask why and how France has deserved the humiliation which presently hangs over her?[72] Was it a crime to have put an end to Austrian influence in Italy and to have changed the despotic regime that ruled the Peninsula for four hundred years? If it was, why did Europe allow France to do it? . . . .

France has every right to attach conditions to her services. This is the A B C of both politics and commerce. I would go further and say that if the rest of Europe approves of the service rendered, and if the debtor is insolvent, Europe becomes the guarantor of the debt and jointly liable for it. Now Italy, so recently emancipated, does not have the necessary strength to look after her own defense. People say that the French army ought to

[71] "We have deserved these ills."

[72] French troops had helped considerably toward the unification of Italy in 1859–60; but French arms since 1849 had also protected papal Rome from Austria and then from the Italian nationalists, and remained there until the collapse of the Second Empire in 1870. One of the reasons for Napoleon III's refusal to accede to the demands of liberal Europe (and of the British Government) was to avoid alienating the Church and Catholic opinion in France—and in the Imperial court. Further, the annexation of Savoy and Nice in 1860 as France's reward for her assistance to Piedmont gave rise to suspicion outside France that Napoleon III had other designs for enlarging his Empire, if need be by conquest. Proudhon felt personally the growing hostility to his country (which was eventually revealed most clearly in the isolation of France during the Franco-Prussian war), and this deepened Proudhon's own "conservatism" and hostility to European liberals, socialists and nationalists.

G*

evacuate Rome sooner rather than later. I accept this. Only it must be understood that if the Austrians take it into their heads to re-enter Rome, France will not stop them. *Italia fara da se.*[73] It would be too much to hope that when we have created Italy and armed it against ourselves, we should then be expected to mount guard and defend it. I accept that France should not claim anything for those who died at Solferino and Magenta, but what should it claim for its protection of Italy?

The Italians are so well aware of this that they have anticipated the reply. "One nation is formed at the expense of another," they say to themselves. "Annexation is the price of unity. If the Emperor of France seizes the left bank of the Rhine from Basle to the sea, and goes back to France's 'natural frontiers,' we ourselves will help him do so. With this addition of eight million souls and six thousand square leagues, France will have re-established her equilibrium."

I would be interested to know what the Belgians, who are so well disposed toward Garibaldi's ideas, think of this system of compensations. I have already heard proposals of the following kind made, sometimes in the name of Italy and sometimes in the name of Poland: that Serbia and Montenegro, and if need be Moldo-Valachia,[74] should be handed over to Austria in exchange for Venice or Galicia. Perhaps Garibaldi has already envisaged something like this. Nothing is more egotistical than nationalism, nothing less scrupulous than the desire for unified government. Much criticism has in recent years been leveled against the outrageous way Europe was divided up by the Congress of Vienna. But if nationalism and unification are given a free hand, much worse things will

[73] The claim of the Italian nationalists that "Italy will go it alone."

[74] The name given at the Conference of Paris of 1858 to what later became Romania.

happen. If the Italian Empire is allowed to complete its formation, you will soon see the French liberal and democratic press do a volte-face and start to examine the possibility of annexing Belgium.[75]

(1862)   *Italy* pp. 122–25

What can I have said in my last letter that you take my sentiments so ill? Do you think that it is French egoism, hatred of liberty, scorn for the Poles and Italians that cause me to mock at and mistrust this commonplace word *nationality*, which is being so widely used and makes so many scoundrels and so many honest citizens talk so much nonsense? For pity's sake, my dear *Kolokol*,[76] do not take offense so easily. If you do, I shall have to say to you what I have been saying for six months about your friend Garibaldi:

"Of great heart, but no brain."[77]

Yes, my dear friend, the *principle of nationality*, which is falsified and contradicted by the laws of war, by people's rights, by history, politics and the laws of progress, is at present quite simply a weapon for war and revolution. This is equally true for Italy, Hungary and Poland. Now I may rightfully wonder whether this weapon is suited to its appointed task, and whether, in the last analysis, it would not be better to abandon this huge farce and, in the interests of liberty and Revolution, return to pure and simple truth or to international law as prescribed by reasons of State and the science of history. This is what I for my part earnestly advocate . . . .

I think I am as well informed as anyone about Italian

[75] This passage helped to get Proudhon expelled from Brussels, where he was then living.

[76] The Russian name of Herzen's newspaper, *The Bell*.

[77] A parody of the lines from La Fontaine's fable "The Fox and the Statue": *Belle-tête, dit-il, Mais de cervelle point.*

affairs, and I affirm that the unitary system now directed against the Pope, Austria and France will not last once Italy has regained her freedom. This unity has been produced by intrigue and I expect only harm to come of it, as I do of anything false and forced. You and your friend Garibaldi may well not share this view, but it is mine, so do not attribute any other to me.

You can see that in Hungary most of the grandees and bourgeois are of the same opinion as myself about their situation. While they are doing their utmost to create liberties and guarantees, they are remaining within the federal system and trying to reject the centralization which the Emperor urges them to accept. They are also supporting the symbol of the Emperor which is their strongest defense against Moscow's Tsarism and France's Caesarism. Might you by any chance favor the Secret Treaty of Tilsit[78] which our two autocrats are trying to re-establish, thus flouting the liberties of the whole of Europe? . . . .

As for Poland, do you know her so little as to believe in her resurrection? Poland has always been the most corrupt of aristocracies and the least disciplined of States. Today all she has to offer is Catholicism and nobility— two very splendid things indeed! Preach *liberty, equality* and *philosophy* to her, help her obtain the constitutional, political and civil liberties which are the characteristic features of our age, and through them prepare her for a more radical revolution which will destroy, along with the large States, all the henceforth groundless distinctions of nationality. But do not talk of these reconstituted nationalities which are in substance a step back into the past, and in form a cup-and-ball game with the aid of which a party of intriguers, going halves with the Tuiler-

[78] Of 1807 between Napoleon I and the Tsar Alexander I, dividing Europe.

ies, Cavour,[79] etc., are trying to avert social revolution.

This, my dear Herzen, is what I think, and these are my politics, and I hope that the best of our democrats will share my views. It seems to me that any other tactics would simply benefit the cause of the despots, and would thrust Europe into a duumvirate of the Holstein-Gottorps[80] and the Bonapartes, and a succession of wars and massacres which for centuries would blot out the little that is left in Europe of the spirit of freedom.

In 1848 politics was put second to economics. In 1851, 1855 and 1859[81] it was the other way around, much to the delight of the French and foreign Jacobins. Now labor is the problem that people are seeking to drown in blood. This is the total success that your great rabble-rouser Garibaldi will have achieved.

(April 21, 1861)   C 11, pp. 22–24

To Alexander Herzen

One of the best things done by the Congress of Vienna was something that the signatory powers had least thought about. It was the intermingling of races and languages which resulted from the irregularity of the geographical divisions that were made. Fraternal relations between the nations were encouraged by the fact that France could count a number of Flemings, Germans, Italians and Basques among its citizens. It would have been even better if not only Belgium, Switzerland, Piedmont, even Prussia and England had had their share of Frenchmen, but also if Austria, Russia, Naples, Spain,

[79] That is, the French Emperor and the Prime Minister of the new Kingdom of Italy.

[80] That is, the Russian Imperial family—in this case the Tsar Alexander II.

[81] 1851, Napoleon III's *coup d'état;* 1855, the Crimean War; 1859, the North Italian Campaign.

Turkey and all the other nations had had a share. Considered in terms of civilization in general, it seemed to be an excellent and inevitable thing, given their large numbers, that the Slav peoples should be divided into several well-balanced powers. Mixtures of this kind were justified by serious considerations, for they taught the people that justice, like religion, rises above distinctions of language, culture and physical characteristics, and that a nation is formed much less by arbitrary geographical boundaries and differences of race than by law.

The principle at first seemed to be justified by the success it encountered . . . .

But once suspicion had been aroused, all this was forgotten. All ideas of fraternization were brushed aside. With lightning rapidity the outlook of the masses took a different course and new idols were forged to replace the gods who had been greeted with such enthusiasm. The treaties of 1815, their compensations, their cross-fertilizations and fusions, were put to one side; even the new constitutions were now discredited. Other principles were set up in opposition to those proclaimed at Vienna. These were more in tune with people's fancies, and were more attractive on account of their materialism. First there was the principle of *nationalities*. This is apparently simple and easy to put into practice, but in reality it is unpredictable, open to exceptions and contradictions, and a source of jealousy and inequality. Secondly there was the highly suspect principle of *natural frontiers,* which is even more arbitrary because it leaves everything to the determination of fate.

(1863)   *Treaties* pp. 389–90

Equilibrium is justice itself. It is people's rights irrespective of so-called natural frontiers and nationalities. If there were no treaties to guarantee this equilibrium, it would re-establish itself of its own accord and no power on earth would be able to prevent it. Once this balancing process had started it would move round the whole of Europe. If France stretched to the Rhine, Russia would reach to Constantinople, Austria to the Balkans and the Black Sea, England to Egypt and elsewhere, and Prussia would include the whole of Germany. This would restore equilibrium in Europe—not, as you might think, despite the Treaties of 1815, but rather as a confirmation of these Treaties, which have the notion of equilibrium as their first principle.

We must admire the way that justice operates once, so to speak, it has been embodied in facts. The situation is such that none of the great powers can accept anything less than the conditions I have just described, but also it is such that none of them will make the corresponding concessions. The Emperor of France could not cede Constantinople to the Russians without belying his family tradition and betraying both France and Europe. In just the same way France, Austria, Greece and Russia cannot leave Egypt and the Suez Canal to the English, who in turn, along with Germany, cannot at any price cede Ostend, Antwerp and the Rhine to France. Thus redrawing the map, which at first sight looked so easy, proves on closer inspection to be impossible.

(1863)   *Treaties* p. 393

I am a republican and I have proved it over the last twelve years . . . . I am a democrat and my repeated explanations of what I mean by anarchy testify to this fact . . . . Finally, I am a socialist, and I have said a hundred times that socialism, so long as it restricts itself to criticizing existing politics and economics and puts forward its hypotheses for criticism, is a form of protest. Insofar as it formulates practical, positive ideas, it is the same thing as social science. Since I am protesting against present society and searching for science, I am, on both scores, a socialist . . . . No, I no more believe in the Triad, the *Circulus* or Metempsychosis[82] than I believe in the resurrection of the dead or constitutional monarchy. I am neither a theist, a pantheist nor an atheist. My only faith, love and hope lie in Liberty and my Country. This is why I am systematically opposed to anything that is hostile to Liberty or foreign to this sacred land of Gaul.[83] I want to see my country return to its original nature, liberated once and for all from foreign beliefs and alien institutions. Our race for too long has been subject to the influence of Greeks, Romans, Barbarians, Jews and Englishmen. They have left us their religion, their laws, their feudal system and their governments . . . . Those of you who accuse me of not being a republican do not truly belong to your land. You have not heard from childhood, as I have, the oak trees of our druidic forests weep for their ancient country. You do not feel your bones, molded with the pure limestone of the Jura, thrill at the memory of our Celtic

[82] Three ideas found in the writings of the French socialist Pierre Leroux.

[83] In French historical debate the racial origins of France revolved around the question of whether there was an original Gallic nation that survived the Frankish invasion of Roman Gaul, or whether the origin of France was in the fusion of these two races. The later eighteenth-century view of the *philosophes* was that the separate races could not be differentiated. The French romantics, however, exalted the Germanic tradition, e.g., Mme. de Staël's *L'Allemagne* of 1810. By the middle of the nineteenth century a reaction had begun against this emphasis on the Germanic influence on French culture and institutions, e.g., in the later writings of the liberal-republican Edgar Quinet, who earlier had been strongly pro-German, and in the nationalist *Action française* movement of the end of the century. The debate had class as well as nationalist implications, since it was argued that the aristocracy was descended from the Frankish-Germanic invaders rather than from the Gauls, who alone were the true *peuple*. Proudhon in this letter takes the side of the Gauls, a position that united both his patriotic feelings and his chosen position as an interpreter of the French working classes.

heroes; Vercingetorix, dragged in the dust of Caesar's triumph, Orgetorix, Ariovistus, and old Galgacus who was vanquished by Agricola. You have not seen liberty appear to you at the brink of our Alpine torrents in the guise of Velleda the Gaul.

You are not children of Brennus. You understand nothing about restoring our nationality. This goes far beyond economic reform and the transformation of a debased society, and appears as the highest aim of the February Revolution. You are on the side of the foreigner. This is why you find liberty, which for our ancestors was the source of all things, so odious. This is why you cannot understand the work to which I have dedicated myself and why you calumniate my intentions. This is why you offer us the Triad, the *Circulus* and the Doctrine.

(December 7, 1849)   *C* 14, pp. 283, 285–86

To Pierre Leroux

But my dear friend, as each day goes by, I am obliged to modify the general tone of my studies in some way.

Old Europe is rushing toward ruin. Immorality and skepticism are competing to destroy society and we can boast that we are witnessing the decay of the Christian nations.

What a downfall it is for France, particularly after a revolution like 1789. We have gone right back to the rule of the sword, the bondage of nations, to unprincipled living and orgies!

It was the Lombardy campaign[84] which set everything in motion. Italy wants to become a unitary state and a great empire. As a consequence, we safeguard our frontier and annex two small provinces. Russia raises no objections and contemplates a similar course of action in the

[84] Of 1859, cf. note 72 above, p. 189.

East. Austria does the same thing on the Danube as England does somewhere else. Prussia sets itself up as the German Empire.

We are heading toward the formation of five or six large empires whose aim is to restore and defend divine right and to exploit the base commoners. The small states are sacrificed in advance, as was previously the case with Poland.

When this happens there will be no law, no liberty, no principles and no morality left in Europe and the great war between the six empires will commence.

What did the Revolution want?

What did the Republic want?

They wanted to avert this age of disaster and shame, and, along with law, liberty and peace, they wanted to bring about the fruitful reign of ideas, labor and morals.

The guilt of Europe will be punished by the armies of Europe. May the execution therefore come swiftly and be over quickly . . . .

The old world with its utopias, its prejudices and its poverty must die, and die ignominiously. Both you and I will live long enough to attend its burial.

(May 3, 1860)   *C* 10, p. 38

To Charles Beslay

Dear friend and fellow countryman. Let me begin by saying straightaway that I do not feel any calling to be the leader of democracy. On the contrary, I think I am destined to be in eternal opposition to its leaders and representatives. Did I do anything different in 1848 and 1849, or even before that, between 1840 and 1848? Well, we are witnessing the same follies, the same political, historical and economic absurdities today, only they are called by different names. Do you really think that the fear of displeasing, the fear of calumny or the regret of seeing this *democratic leadership* pass into the hands of charlatan mediocrities, could induce me to change my course and my plans? . . . . Our nation has been in a state of decadence for *thirty years.* I am sometimes told that people's minds are awakening and their consciousnesses beginning to stir, but in the light of the last ten years, during which our people have tasted shame, I foresee nothing but more decadence if I judge the future by the false ideas that are currently held in France and shared by so many honest citizens . . . .

Can you believe that a man who is in advance of his times may be thought right and enjoy popularity? Let me tell you, dear friend, that the most backward and retrograde element in any country is the mass, or what you call democracy. Of course this is what I am working for. But I know what it is and what it is worth, and I would take good care not to lose its case before reason and history by defending it as it would like me to defend it. I repeat that, from the point of view of principles, democracy has no worse enemy than itself. I dare to hope, since my career is getting on, that it will not one day reproach me for having sacrificed its true interests to utopias.

(October 12, 1861)   *C* 11, pp. 220–22

To Mr. X***

You are perfectly right, my dear friend, in all that you have said to me about *democracy,* and you need have no fear that I will forget or take back what I have said. Moreover I am glad that you have reminded me of it, for this is a proof that there have been changes in people's thinking since the *coup d'état.*[85] The *democrats* no longer believe in their own principles and would no longer dare to swear by the sovereignty or *kratia* of the people. Conse-

[85] Of 1851, establishing Napoleon III's Empire.

quently I need not fear their opposition in this sphere. But we do have to reckon with words, habits and situations . . . .

The word *democracy,* which has lost its real meaning, is accepted as almost synonymous with the republic. It has been accepted by such men as de Tocqueville who by no means admire popular wisdom. For us it still means that, even if we are not working toward the omnipotence of the masses, we are working toward their emancipation through law and liberty, and consequently we are defending their interests.

However much I may misuse the plebs and *democrats,* and whatever ill I may speak of this *kratia,* I cannot oppose them. Now, this is what I would be doing if, to very little effect, I were to proscribe one word. Readers do not like having constantly to use new dictionaries, and it is easier to get them to accept any number of reservations, criticisms and amendments, than the use of a different word. They will know that my brand of democracy is not the same as that of the democrats, and they will readily accept the distinction. But they would not also accept a change of cockade, for this would look very like division.

I have similar observations to make, and with more reason, about the word *revolution,* but I will leave you to think about them. I would go even further and say that I must uphold the higher idea or *spirit* of revolution, although I am not what is commonly called a revolutionary, that is to say a *disruptive element.* The revolution of '89 marks the beginning of a new age of history and law. It is true that it was betrayed, misunderstood and deformed by the so-called revolutionaries. This will emerge more and more clearly in my writings, which will increase in number during the next few years.

Furthermore, *Revolution* means preservation as well as destruction.[86] It is a crisis similar to that which separates

[86] Cf. Section xi above for Proudhon's views on Revolution.

different ages in the life of the individual. It renews, re-invigorates, purges, fortifies and rejuvenates. It is true that if it is not well guided, or is in the hands of ignorant, brutal leaders, it does as much harm as good. What can be done about this? It is neither my fault, nor the fault of revolution.

All in all, and reserving the right to explain myself frankly, as I will never fail to do, I consider that there would be very little to be gained from making a profession of faith which would result in my abandoning certain terms once and for all, and I think the disadvantages would be considerable. In my next work to be published, on Poland,[87] I will say that my turn has now come to call myself a *conservative* and *to defend the institution of property*. In fact I have already hinted at this in my pamphlet on literary property.[88] This will not prevent me from remaining what I will always be, namely, an interpreter of the *Revolution,* a *republican,* a *democrat* even, and a *socialist* into the bargain. A word to the wise is enough. In the course of time, words, like institutions, change their meaning. Constitutional monarchy is not at all the same thing as monarchy at the time of the Hebrews. Must we, as a result, ban the word monarch? We may own land in five or six different ways. Should we therefore ban the word *property?* We must introduce the notion of MOVEMENT into our way of thinking, not attack the words themselves.

(March 4, 1862)   C 12, pp. 7–8

To Doctor Cretin

You also know that, after having been the most revolutionary spirit of my time, it is my ambition to become THE MOST CONSERVATIVE.

[87] This work was never finished; his *Federal Principle* grew out of his studies on Poland and Italy.
[88] Cf. note 42 above, p. 126.

The publication of my book *War and Peace* and my *Memoir on Taxation* will be the start of the fulfillment of this ambition, which I hope has your approval since you understand what I really mean.

(May 21, 1861)   C 11, p. 82

To Charles Beslay

Probably the immediate result [of the publication of *War and Peace*] will be a slating from the Jacobin press. But their party is falling into discredit, and in return I will obtain the support of all who are moderate, conciliatory, friends of order and *conservative*. I predict that a few years from now, after having been the most revolutionary spirit of my time, I will become the most conservative, by virtue, precisely, of my revolutionary ideas. The world revolves in this way, and if I have shown any intelligence, it is in having observed this movement so correctly.

(May 21, 1861)   C 11, p. 85

To Mathey

XIV   WAR AND PEACE

The Phenomenology of War

War is divine, that is to say it is primordial, essential to life and to the production of men and society. It is deeply seated in human consciousness and its idea embraces all human relationships. When history began mankind revealed and expressed his noblest faculties through war: religion, justice, poetry, the fine arts, economics, politics, government, nobility, bourgeoisie, royalty, property. In subsequent ages war retempered morals, maintained the balance of power between States, aided progress, established the reign of justice and guaranteed liberty. Let us imagine for a moment that we can get rid of the idea of war. Nothing remains of either humanity's past or present existence. We cannot conceive of what society could have been like without it; we cannot guess what it might become. Civilization topples into the void. Its former existence becomes a myth that does not correspond to any reality, and its future development is an unknown quantity that no philosophy could define.

(1861) *War* p. 23

War stems from our consciousness in the same way as religion and justice. Heroes are inspired by the same spontaneous zeal as prophets and lovers of justice. That is why war is divine . . . .

War, we greet you! It was war that enabled man to assert his majesty and valor when he had scarcely emerged from the primeval slime which served him as a womb. He first dreamed of glory and immortality as he stood over the body of an enemy he had slain. Our philanthropic souls are horrified by this blood which is spilled so freely and by fratricidal carnage. I am afraid that this squeamishness may indicate that our virtue is failing in strength. What is so terrible in supporting a great cause in heroic combat, at the risk of killing or being killed, if both sides are equally honorable and their claims equally just? What is there so particularly immoral about it? Death is the crown of life. How could man, who is a thinking, moral, free being, have a more noble end?

Wolves and lions do not make war on each other any more than sheep and beavers. This fact has for a long time been used to satirize our species. Why do people not see that, on the contrary, this is the sign of our greatness; that if, to imagine the impossible, nature had made man as an exclusively industrious, sociable being, and not at all warlike, he would from the first moment have sunk to the level of the beasts whose destiny is limited to a purely collective existence? Why can they not see that he would have lost his faculties for revolution along with his proud heroism, that most marvelous and most fertile of all his faculties? If our lives were simply communal, civilization would be no more than a stable. Would we appreciate the value of peoples and races? Would we progress? Would we even have the notion of *valeur*[89] which has passed from the language of chivalry into the language of commerce? All peoples who have gained a certain measure of renown boast first and foremost of their military history, for this is their greatest claim to fame in posterity. Will you hold this against them as a mark of infamy? Philanthropists talk of abolishing war; they should take care lest in so doing they degrade the human race.

(1861)   *War* pp. 31–32

Action is the principal condition of life, health and strength in an organized being. Action enables it to develop and increase its faculties and to fulfill its destiny.

The same is true of the thinking, moral, free being. Activity is the essential condition of his existence, meaning of course intelligent, moral action since I am talking about the spheres of the intellect and morality.

Now, what is action?

For there to be action, whether physical, intellectual or moral, there must be some ground that exists in relation to the acting subject, a non-self that confronts the self as ground and subject of action and that resists and opposes the acting self. Action, therefore, is a struggle. To act is to fight.

[89] *Valeur* in French has the double meaning of both "valor" and "value."

Since man is an organized, thinking, moral, free being, he therefore struggles first of all with nature. That is to say, his relationship with it is one of action and reaction. In this sphere alone he has many opportunities for displaying his courage, patience, scorn of death, devotion to his own glory and to the happiness of his fellow creatures, in short, his virtue.

But man's dealings are not with nature alone. In his path he also meets men; men who are his equals, his rivals for the possession of the world and the support of his fellow men, men who compete with him, thwart him, and, as sovereign, independent powers, impose their *veto* on him. This is both inevitable and desirable.

I say on the one hand that this is inevitable because it is impossible for there ever to be complete agreement between two beings who are progressing along the path of knowledge and consciousness but who are not walking in step, between two beings whose viewpoints on all questions are different and whose interests are increasingly opposed. Their meeting will inevitably result in a divergence of opinion, in opposing principles, in polemics and the clash of ideas.

I add on the other hand that this is desirable. It is from divergences of opinion, and the antagonism that this engenders, that a new world, higher than the organic, speculative, effective world, is created. It is the world of social dealings, of law, liberty, politics and morals. But before dealings are possible, strife is inevitable; before the peace treaty there is the duel and war. This is true of each moment of existence.

True human virtue is not merely negative. It does not simply mean abstaining from everything which law and morality condemn. It consists much more of offering energetic opposition through talent, will and strength of character to people who by their very existence try to blot us out. *Sustine et abstine,* said the Stoic. Sustain, that is to say fight, resist, be strong, vanquish. This is the first and most important principle in life; *hoc est primum et maximum mandatum*. Abstain is the second. Where will this duel lead? In certain cases, the nations reply, it will lead to the death of one of the parties. And this is not unjust, perfidious or outrageous. It is simply the result of the natural law that prescribes struggle, even by force of arms, and even in some cases to the death, as a condition of life and virtue. It is the warrior who insults his enemy, who uses unlawful weapons or dishonorable methods, who is called a criminal fighter, a murderer.

Thus war is an integral part of human life and must endure as long as humanity endures. It is a part of man's moral code, regardless of the forms it takes, of the rules of combat, of the decisions as to the *rights* of the victor and *obligations* of the vanquished. Not only is war not disappearing but, like everything pertaining to human affairs, its forms and methods change with the times. Like a fire that does not go out until it lacks fuel, or like human life that does not fail until it is deprived of nourishment, war spreads and increases in gravity in proportion to the religious, philosophical, political and industrial development of the nations. It seems that nothing can extinguish war except the extinction of morality itself. The organic, natural causes that foster our spirit of contradiction and antagonism also see to it that this antagonism is perpetuated, and that it grows in proportion to our knowledge and development, to the number of interests involved, to the passions which are in conflict, to the pride which is at stake . . . .

Let us therefore conclude, with the mystics Ancillon, de Maistre and Portalis, and with the materialist Hobbes —but also in the name of a higher reason which is beyond both mysticism and materialism—that war in one form or another is essential to mankind and that it is a vital condition of our social and moral life. Putting aside the modifications in form and method introduced by scientific and moral progress, war is as much a feature of civilized living as it is of barbarian existence, and is, from all these points of view, the most splendid form of individual and social life. Strength, bravery, virtue, heroism, the sacrifice of possessions, liberty and life and of what is even more precious than life itself, the joys of love and family life, rest earned from toil, intellectual and civic honors, all these are things which war brings out in us and are the heights of virtue to which it beckons.

(1861)   *War* pp. 54–56

To me it is clear that war is linked at a very deep level, and in a way we are only just beginning to perceive, with man's sense of religion, justice, beauty and morality. One might even say that it is the abstract formulation of the dialectic. War is the basis of our history, our life and our whole being. It is, I repeat, everything. People speak of abolishing war as they might of local taxes or customs duties. They do not see that if one takes away war and everything related to it, nothing, absolutely nothing, of man's past remains, and not an atom is left on which to build the future. I would ask these inept peacemakers, as I myself was once asked in connection with property: What sort of society do you envisage once you have abolished war? What notions and beliefs will it hold? What forms of literature, poetry and art will it produce? What will you make of man, who is an intelligent, religious, lawmaking, free, individual being, and who because of all these things is also a fighter? What will you do with the nation, which is an independent, growing, autonomous collective force? What, in this state of permanent siesta, will become of mankind?

(1861)   *War* pp. 71–72

This is the correction I propose to add to my works on *War and Peace* and on *Justice*.

The facts in both works are sound and accurately presented, and their meaning is correct, but one thing is missing. What I must do is make the works complement each other by showing that *Labor* and *War,* which are contrary and incompatible, are two correlative terms that express the same law and reveal the same morality and destiny. This way of looking at facts, by nature so opposed and irreconcilable, is supported by all the exegeses of the ancients as well as by modern philosophy, particularly that of Hegel.

If in my works on *Justice* and *War and Peace* certain expressions appear to be too absolute or too excessive, it is of course the case that the meaning of these expressions must be modified in the way I have just suggested. All the more so since the author knows as well as anyone else that because society is in a state of continuous evolution, although following an immutable law, truth can never be reached in its broadest, most general or more absolute formulation.

It would give me great pleasure, my dear Monsieur Clerc, if this explanation were to satisfy you as well as it satisfies me. It is some time since I observed the constant mobility of truth which the semi-philosophers call deceit, either on the part of Providence, or of our own understanding. In fact it is simply the ceaseless, polymorphous revelation of truth itself. Would not making accusations against various phases in human activity mean indicting the diversities of nature itself? Is nature lying because Being sometimes takes animal, sometimes vegetable and sometimes mineral or gaseous form? Would it, do you think, be more truthful if it were reduced simply to a homogeneous, uniform, immobile mass? Would you have more faith in the *rudis indigestaque moles*[90] of before

---

[90] "A rough, unordered shapeless mass," Ovid, *Metamorphoses,* I, 7; Proudhon was seemingly fond of this passage, cf. note 60 above, p. 166.

Creation than in the earthly paradise of the seventh day?
(March 4, 1863)   C 12, pp. 341–42

To Clerc

The Economic Resolution of Conflict

Our fundamental proposition is that the primary cause
of all disruption and war is endemic to society, and that
this cause is poverty. Nations and corporations, individuals
and governments, commoners and nobles, proletarians
and princes—all suffer hardship. Scarcity dogs us every
moment. If heads of State slacken the reins for one instant, the peoples will surge forward. No blood or
treasure will be too costly for them to spend on destroying
each other and on impoverishing themselves still further.
This is why, once the blaze has been started, historians
and political writers do not really have to look for its
causes. The only question that need be asked is how
the monster broke its chains, what intrigue or necessity
of fate, what blunder on the part of those in authority,
enabled it to throw itself upon the world? . . . .

The discoveries made by the navigators have for four
centuries been providing the various European powers
with numerous sources of profit and vast overflow areas for
their populations. The settlements established in the two
Americas, Africa, Australia and the South Sea Islands
have been a considerable factor in maintaining peace in
the world. But this cannot go on much longer. Soon all
the corners of the world will have been developed. Everywhere the land has been taken over. What were once
the most deserted regions are now being filled with colo-
nists from Europe, who at once turn against their mother
countries and are ready to take up arms against them.
What is there left to conquer on the globe? ... The
day when India, Australia, the South Sea Islands and

Africa, all the countries which today are being exploited by Europeans, will have proclaimed or regained their independence, when, as sovereign possessors of their own wealth, they raise the price of their commodities and compete with our own products, demanding equal returns for all that they provide, that day all the nations of the world will find that they are obstacles to each other and will be forced back into a state of poverty. When that happens, if no sort of balance between production and consumption is established, if the increase in population continues to outstrip industry, the struggle will break out (there being no lack of political motives), and it will be inexorable and universal.

(1861) *War* pp. 381–83

God forbid that I should preach the gentle virtues and joys of peace to my fellow men! I too am a man, and what I like most in man is the bellicose temperament that puts him above all authority and love, as well as above fatalism, and through which he makes it clear that *he* is the legitimate sovereign of the earth, that it is *he* who can penetrate the meaning of things, that it is *he* who is a free being. I would simply like to observe that war, in this day and age, whatever its origins, cannot be started without the aggressor's being subject to foul suspicion, and that there are no longer any methods that make it feasible.

My first point was that the real cause of war can no longer be hidden, and that all the political grounds which cover it up look suspiciously like empty words. This is true both of the masses and of governments. Would England, for example, go to war to defend a principle or an idea? Indeed not! England is merely concerned about what M. de Fiquelmont has called *exploitation,* unless of course anyone is threatening to invade her shores. Now, all nations share England's feeling to a greater or lesser extent; all do their best to imitate her policy of exploitation. The years 1814–15 that ushered in the age of constitutional government in Europe are also, and for the same reason, those that saw the growth to dominance of material interests. In this the masses follow the lead of the government. Like the bourgeoisie, the proletariat only values liberty and its results for the profit they hope to gain, as should have been made clear to everyone by the events of 1848 and the morals of 1852.

The spirit of cupidity and greed is the true characteristic of the present epoch. The poor exploit the rich, the worker his employer, the tenant and the farmer their landlord, the entrepreneur his shareholders, just as much as the capitalist exploits and grinds down the industrialist, the landlord the cultivator of his land, and the manufacturer his wage-earners . . . .

Such a system cannot go on. Egoism, dishonesty, scorn for man and for principles, have been set up as maxims and idolized. These idols have been subject to criticism for a long time, and we know the cost of worshipping them. One thing, at least, is certain—namely, that politics has been revealed for what it is, and that if war were to become widespread and its real cause to be seen, it would be a return to cannibalism of the most horrific kind. We have already had a foretaste of this in the way the insurrection of June 1848 was repressed.

Whether we put it briefly or at length, it looks as if war, even between the most honorable of nations and whatever its officially declared motives, can never be anything other than war fought in the name of exploitation and property—in other words, class war. Until a just economic system has been established between both nations and individuals, war has no further function on earth. When political power is subject to economic power, the law of force is temporarily abrogated . . . .

War was simply aiming at the grouping and balancing of political forces. What we must do now is organize economic forces. What use would war and its bloody tribunal be in helping to solve this new problem?

(1861)   *War* pp. 464–66

It becomes clear to anyone who makes a careful study of the history of war that mankind tends not to extinguish but to transform antagonism into what it has always been conventional to term PEACE . . . .

The aim of war is to determine which of two disputing parties holds the prerogative of force. It is a struggle between two forces, not their destruction; it is a struggle between men, not their extermination. It must not, outside the conflict itself and the subsequent political changes, in any way interfere with persons or property . . . .

It follows that antagonism, which we accept as a law of man and of nature, does not essentially take the form of physical fighting or wrestling. It can equally well be a contest in the sphere of industry or progress. This really comes to the same thing as far as the spirit of war is concerned. "Let the most valiant gain dominion," says war. "Amen," reply labor, industry and economics. What constitutes the valor of a man or a nation? Is it not intelligence, virtue, strength of character, knowledge, industry, labor, wealth, sobriety, liberty and devotion to country? Did not the great captain say that in war moral strength is to physical strength as three is to one? Do not the rules of war and the code of chivalry also teach us that in combat we must seek honor and refrain from wrongdoing, treachery, plunder and marauding? Let us therefore fight, but in order to do this we do not need to attack each other with bayonets or to shoot at each other. Just as law, which at first was exclusively personal, became realty or property law through war, so war also must cease to be personal and become exclusively a matter of things. This does not mean that in these new battles we will not have

to give proof of resolution and devotion, or scorn death
and ease. We will still have to count the wounded and
the dead. All cowardice, weakness, vulgarity and faint-
heartedness must still expect to be rewarded by servitude,
forfeiture of esteem and by misery. Poor pay, poverty and
beggary, such being the utmost degree of shame, await
the defeated.

Thus the transformation of antagonism is a result of its
nature, its development and its law. It is also a result of
its aim. In fact the aim of antagonism is not simply destruction, unproductive consumption or extermination for
the sake of extermination. Its aim is to create an ever
higher order and endless perfection. Seen in this light, it
is clear that labor offers antagonism a far wider and far
richer field of activity than war.

(1861) *War* pp. 482–83

To sum up, it is quite legitimate to postulate a condition
of perpetual, universal peace. This is contained within the
law of antagonism, within the whole phenomenon of
war, in the contradiction we have pointed out between
the declared, legal notion of war and its economic cause,
in the ever-increasing role which labor is playing in running societies, and finally in the progress which has been
made in LAW, the law of force, international law, political
law, civil law, economic law. War has been the symbol,
peace the realization. The setting up of laws between
men constitutes the very abolition of war and signifies
the organizing of peace. All nations have welcomed this
promise. They have all dreamed of turning their swords
into plowshares and their spears into pruning hooks.
Hitherto the world has known only temporary peace. The
last two centuries have seen the peace of Westphalia, the
peace of Nijmegen, the peace of Utrecht, the peace of
Aix-la-Chapelle, the peace of Amiens, the peace of Tilsit

and the peace of Vienna.[91] What we want today is THE PEACE. The world understands and desires no other.

In what conditions may we obtain this organized peace, whose clauses cannot be laid down by any one nation and which, since it is founded on the regulated struggle between forces, is beyond the reach of all the armies in the world?

It is not by subscriptions and meetings, federations, amphictyonies, or congresses, as Abbé de Saint-Pierre[92] thought, that peace will become a serious reality beyond the reach of any attack. Statesmen are as powerless to insure this as philosophers. The Holy Alliance failed to do it, and no philanthropic propaganda can be of any use. A peace which is signed at sword point is never anything more than a truce. A peace drawn up by a council of economists and Quakers would simply be a joke, like the famous Baiser Lamourette.[93] The workers alone are capable of putting an end to war by creating economic equilibrium. This presupposes a radical revolution in ideas and morals.

(1861) *War* p. 487

XV ART

The critical school says: "Until the present day, art has only concerned itself with gods, heroes, and saints, and it is high time that it concerned itself with mere mortals.

[91] Proudhon lists here some of the main European peace treaties between 1648 and 1815.

[92] The Abbé Saint-Pierre published in 1713 a *Project for a Perpetual Peace*.

[93] That is, a short-lived peace; from the kisses of peace that Lamourette moved the different factions of the Assembly to exchange in 1792.

By idealizing, symbolizing and seeking for models above man's condition and destiny, it has finished by creating a tissue of fantasies; it has got lost in the void." But, you will say, what can art do with such as we who are a wretched, servile, ignoble, uncouth, ugly mob? It could do something most interesting, the most glorious thing of all. Its task is to improve us, help us and save us. In order to improve us it must first of all know us, and in order to know us, it must see us as we are and not in some fantastic, reflected image which is no longer us. Thanks to the critical school, man will become his own mirror, and he will learn how to contemplate his soul through studying his true countenance.

(1865)   *Art* p. 310

As for me, I confess I abhor all lies, fantasy, conventions, all allegory, hypocrisy and flattery in painting, as much as in politics and literary style. I do not want to flatter the masses any more than I want to flatter princes. And if, as everyone knows, it is true that we are living in an age of decadence, in which civic courage has been annihilated, personal virtue cast aside, the race trodden down, all sentiments falsified and depraved, I maintain that instead of hiding these things we must begin by speaking out and seeing things as they really are. Otherwise we are making fools of ourselves. What we need is a dose of cod liver oil and all we are offered is sugar and water. Ours is an age with an enormous police force but lacking principles or morals. It is calm on the surface but underneath, revolutionary. The same must be true of art . . . .

It is to Courbet's[94] credit that he is the first painter who, by imitating Molière's comic genius in the theater,

---

[94] Proudhon and Courbet were good friends, and discussed parts of this book together.

has seriously tried to warn us, chasten us and improve us through portraying us as we really are; who, instead of amusing us with fables or flattering us by adding a lot of bright colors, has had the courage to depict us not as nature intended us to be, but as our passions and our vices have made us.

It is no good saying to him, "Waken this pretty little gossip; send an electric shock through her body and make it a little slimmer. Lighten her brow and give her lips a smile of intelligence. If you do this your spinning girl[95] will be worth fifteen thousand francs instead of fifteen hundred, and you will enter the ranks of the Academicians." . . . .

This is what Courbet would reply: If I were to do this it would be fantasy, idealization, or in effect, given the state of our morals, a form of prostitution. Consider, if you will, that nowadays true human beauty is to be found in our midst only in pain and suffering, and very seldom in our petty feelings. This is why my women who weep at *The Burial* are beautiful, and it cost me dearly, I assure you, to paint them in that way. This is why my *Dying Duellist* is so handsome, why my young people who exchange *frank looks of love* as they return from the fair are interesting, and it is why the *Empire Demoiselle*,[96] who is totally abandoned to Venus and burning with desire, seeming to want to devour the very grass, retains a glimmer of beauty. The very strength of her passion restores to her a trace of the dignity which has been ravaged

[95] *The Sleeping Spinner,* 1853, for which the model was Courbet's sister Zélie.

[96] Proudhon is referring to the subjects rather than to the customary titles for these last three paintings: the first is *The Wounded Man,* 1844; the second, *The Peasants of Flagey Returning from the Fair,* 1850—the same year as the *Burial at Ornans;* the third, *Young Women on the Banks of the Seine,* 1857, which caused something of a scandal when it was first exhibited since the two figures are unmistakably courtesans.

by vice. You quote the Dutch and the Flemish, who in their village fairs, their wedding festivities, their gatherings, their household interiors and even in their taverns are always cheerful; you say they are both pleasing and amusing. Doubtless. But this simply proves once again what I have just said, namely, that the artist's only material comes from true observation. The painters of these works saw before them a gay, wealthy, cheerful society. They were happier than we are. Do you know who the painter has as his models today? Avarice, gambling, pride, lust, greedy indolence, ruthlessness in using others and prostitution. I can only restore to the public what I am lent. It is not my fault if people recoil at the sight of their own image.

(1865)   *Art* pp. 316–17, 319–20

PART THREE

Philosophy and Morality

XVI RELIGION

"If God did not exist," said Voltaire, the enemy of religions, "it would be necessary to invent him." . . . .

"I thought formerly," said Rousseau, "that one could
be a just man without God, but I have since recognized
my error." His is basically the same reasoning as Voltaire's,
the same justification of intolerance: man does good and
abstains from evil only because there is a Providence
watching him, and cursed be those who deny it. Moreover, and this is the height of illogicality, the very man
who demands a rewarding and avenging Divinity as the
sanction for virtue is the same man who teaches as a tenet
of faith that man is innately good.

For my part I say that the first duty of the thinking,
free man is ceaselessly to banish the idea of God from his
mind and consciousness. For God, if he exists, is essentially
hostile to our nature and we in no way depend upon his
authority. We acquire knowledge in spite of him, well-
being in spite of him, and social existence in spite of him.
Each step in our progress represents one more victory in
which we annihilate the Deity.

Let no one continue to say that the ways of God are
impenetrable! For we have penetrated them, and we have
seen proof of God's impotence, if not of his ill will, written
in letters of blood. My reason, so long kept under, is rising
little by little to reach the infinite. In time I shall become less and less a perpetrator of misfortune, and
through the enlightenment of my understanding and the
perfecting of my liberty I shall purify myself, idealize
my being and become the lord of creation and the equal

H*

of God. One single instant of disorder, which the Almighty could have prevented but did not, is an accusation against his providential care and reveals the imperfection of his wisdom. The smallest step forward that man—ignorant, forsaken and betrayed—takes toward the good, honors him beyond measure. By what right could God still say to me: "Be holy even as I am holy"? "Lying spirit," I would reply, "thou foolish God, thy reign is past. Seek new victims among the beasts. I know that I am not, nor ever can be holy, and how canst thou be if I am made in thine image? Eternal father, Jupiter, Jehovah, we have learned to know thy ways. Thou art, thou wast, and ever wilt be, the envier of Adam and the tormentor of Prometheus."

Thus I do not fall into the fallacy that was refuted by St. Paul when he forbade the vessel to say to the potter: "Why hast thou made me thus?" I do not reproach the author of all things for having made me a creature of disharmony, an incoherent assembly, for I could not exist save on this condition. I am content to cry: Why dost thou deceive me? Why, by thy silence, hast thou unleashed egoism within me? Why hast thou subjected me to the torture of universal doubt through the bitter illusion that arises out of the conflicting ideas thou hast set in my understanding? Doubt of the truth, doubt of justice, doubt of my consciousness and my liberty, doubt of thyself, O God. Because of my doubt I am necessarily at war with myself and with my neighbor. This, supreme Father, is what thou hast done for our happiness and thy glory. This is what thy will and thy government have been from the beginning. This is the bread, kneaded with blood and with tears, with which thou hast fed us. Thou thyself hast made us commit the faults for which we ask forgiveness. Thou thyself hast laid the snares from which we beg thee to deliver us. Thou thyself art the Satan who besets us.

Thou wast exultant, and none dared gainsay thee when, after thou hadst tormented in body and soul the righteous Job, the image of our humanity, thou didst insult his candid piety, his modest and respectful ignorance. We were as nothing before thine invisible majesty, to whom we ascribed the sky for canopy and the earth for footstool. And now thou art unthroned and shattered. Thy name, for so long the scholar's final argument, the judge's sanction, the prince's power, the poor man's hope, the shelter of the repentant sinner, this same incommunicable name, henceforth destined to be cursed and scorned, will be hissed at among men. God is stupidity and cowardice; God is hypocrisy and falsehood; God is tyranny and poverty; God is evil. For as long as men bow before altars, mankind will remain damned, the slave of kings and priests. As long as one man receives another man's oath in God's name, society will be founded on perjury, and peace and love will be banished from among mortals. Get thee hence, O God. For from this day forward, cured of my fear of thee and grown wise, I swear, with my hand stretched out to heaven, that thou art nothing but the executioner of my reason, the ghost of my consciousness.

I therefore deny God's supremacy over humanity. I reject his providential rule, for its nonexistence has been sufficiently proved by man's metaphysical and economic hallucinations, in a word, by the martyrdom of our kind. I do not accept the Supreme Being's jurisdiction over man. I will strip him of his titles of father, king, judge, good, clement, merciful, helper, rewarder and avenger. All these attributes which make up the idea of Providence are simply a caricature of man's attributes. They are irreconcilable with mankind's autonomy, and moreover they are given the lie by civilization's history of aberrations and catastrophes.

(1846) *Econ. Contrads.* I, pp. 382–84

Man is destined to live without religion.[97] A whole host of signs proves that through some inner working society always tends to free itself from this outer shell that has become useless.

(1843)   *Creation* p. 63

Religion exists, not as the unbelievers of old maintained, with the deliberate intention of subjugating mankind (although this was in fact what happened) but in order to provide an authoritative basis for Justice, without which society cannot survive.

We can thus see how trivial it is to contest, as the Protestants do, the legitimacy of the Church of Rome, the soundness of its tradition, the truth of its teaching, the variants of its dogma, the purity of its discipline, the modifications of its history and the uncertainties of its exegesis. It is equally trivial to contest, as do the deists, the truth of the prophecies and miracles, the mission of Moses, the messianic role of Christ and so on. To do this is to behave like the Pharisees of the Gospels whom

[97] This assertion should cause no alarm, given the distinction I have made between the moral *law* and the religious *symbol*. The former is eternal and absolute, the latter variable and transitory, its only function being to provide morality with a temporary basis and sanction. Now, the new science must replace religion in everything, and must do better than its predecessors. Only on this condition will the conclusions I am going to draw be legitimate. Thus let the fearful take heart. Who in any case today would dare to attack the moral law, but who, on the other hand, is worried about symbols? Do fathers send their children to catechism classes so that they can learn how to theologize, or is it not rather to learn the principles of integrity and good manners? This is the crux of the matter. (Proudhon's footnote.)

Christ rebuked for straining at a gnat and swallowing a camel.

One can also see how irrational and hypocritical it is for a society that claims to be religious to try to separate the spiritual from the temporal and separate the Church from the State. It is like giving a lame man crutches to walk with and then making him carry them on his back.

(1858)   Justice I, pp. 320–21

The hour for a religion has struck when the troubled conscience asks not whether that particular religion is true, for doubts about dogma are not sufficient to destroy a religion; not whether it needs reforming, for reform in matters of faith is proof of a religion's vitality; but whether that religion, which for so long has been seen as the safeguard and stay of morality, is in fact equal to the task: in other words, whether it really constitutes a moral law . . . .

I reply sadly, like the President of the Convention pronouncing Louis XVI guilty: "No, Christianity has no moral law, and, moreover, it cannot have one" ... Since therefore, after eighteen centuries of existence, the Christian Church finds itself in the same situation as after two thousand years of existence did the polytheistic church, which perished because it had no moral law, it is lost.

(1858)   Justice I, p. 393

XVII   DIALECTIC

All ideas are coeternal within universal logic. They appear to be successive only in history, when one after another they come to the fore and take over the direction of affairs. In logic the operation by which one idea is deposed is termed *negation,* and that by which another idea establishes itself, *affirmation.*

(1851) *Revn.* p. 186

Principles are the soul of history. Modern philosophy holds it as axiomatic that everything has its own idea, and consequently its own principle and law; that every fact has its corresponding idea; and that everything in the universe is the expression of an idea. This is as true of the rolling stone as it is of the flower and the butterfly. Ideas stir up chaos and render it fertile. Ideas guide humanity through revolutions and catastrophes.

(1861) *War* pp. 9–10

Reason's task is to embrace in a single perspective ideas that in substance, cause, origin or form are totally disparate, and to arrange them into a single series of equal or identical terms.

Dialectical Series will be the name I give to this series, the product of reasoning, which can compare terms that are otherwise totally incomparable. *Serial Dialectic* is the name I will give to the special theory that teaches how to apply it . . . .

In the REALITY Series there is an essence, a something that resists, that struggles to remain unchanged and would rather be destroyed than undergo any metamorphosis or the smallest alteration. It is something more than just weight, color, movement, shape or series. It is in fact something beyond man's understanding.[98]

(1843) *Creation* pp. 193, 286

[98] It seems that the author means that creatures of all the natural kingdoms, although we know them only in series and as series, are nevertheless something more than just ideas. The

My studies on economic reform in the period 1848–
1851 dealt particularly with the *objective* side of the problem. At the time we were being drowned in Christian socialist and communistic sentimentalism,[99] and the solution to the problem of the proletariat was presented as
needing only a little preaching and propaganda. When
once they had been sufficiently sermonized and evangel-
ized, it seemed as if the Jews[100] and the Philistines would

---

proof, he adds, that these objects are not simply ideas, is that
they do not allow themselves to be handled, made and un-
made, composed, dismantled and recomposed at will, which is
what characterizes ideas. Any intellectual operation can very
well be transformed into a different one. What is demonstrated by a syllogism can very well be proved by induction
or series and vice versa without the truth or the conclusion of
the operation being affected in any way. Why should this be
so? Because what is being analyzed is simply an idea. Although
the intelligence may conceive *a priori* of the possibility of dis-
secting an animal and then bringing it back to life, just as one
may take a clock to pieces and put it together again, experiment
shows that this is impossible. Thus, the author concludes,
and we quite agree with him, the animal is something more
than an idea.

According to my ideo-realist theory, the reality of being increases progressively from the mineral world to the vegetable
world, from the vegetable world to the animal kingdom, and
from the animal kingdom to man. It reaches its highest peak in
SOCIETY, which is the freest organization and least tolerant of
the arbitrariness of those who govern it. This is precisely the
opposite of what is commonly supposed. (Proudhon's footnote)

[99] Cf. note 12 above, p. 58.

[100] Proudhon is not the only socialist writer of this period
to use the term "Jews" derogatively as being equivalent to
bankers and financiers. Of itself this might not seem to be any
more anti-Semitic than *The Merchant of Venice,* but Proudhon's diaries (*Carnets,* ed. P. Haubtmann, Marcel Rivière,
Paris, 1960 to date) reveal that he had almost paranoid feelings
of hatred against the Jews. In 1847 he considered publishing

spontaneously give up their wealth and become leaders and helpers in the egalitarian movement.

In the third section of my book JUSTICE [*in the Revolution and the Church*], entitled *Goods*, I re-examined all these questions from the more detached viewpoint that I had not had time to achieve in the inevitable heat of a period of revolutionary struggle. In the earlier chapter of *Justice* I had formulated the great principle that Justice is immanent in human affairs, and this was the criterion by which I set out to judge all institutions. There for the first time I looked in depth at the notion of the legitimation of private property from the subjective angle—that of the owner of property . . . .

What distinguished this study, *Goods*, from my previous publications on property was that in it I put forward the idea of making property morally acceptable by making Justice an integral part of it, without there being any adverse effects on the economic consequences I had elabo-

---

both a reply to Marx's *The Poverty of Philosophy* and an article against the Jewish race, which he said he "hated." The proposed article would have "Called for the expulsion of the Jews from France, except for those married to Frenchwomen; the abolition of all their synagogues; the denial to them of all employment; the abolition of their cult . . . . The Jew is the enemy of the human race. This race must be sent back to Asia, or exterminated. H. Heine, A. Weil, and others are simply secret spies. Rothschild, Crémieux, Marx, Fould, evil, choleric, envious, bitter men, etc., etc., who hate us" (*Carnets*, vol. 2, p. 337: No. VI, 178). Although Proudhon never refers to the book, his attitude to the Jews is comparable to Alphonse Toussenel's extended development of the association between Jews and finance in *The Jews, Kings of the Epoch: The Financial Feudalism*, first published in 1845. It is usually regarded as one of the first works of anti-Semitism in the modern sense. This same association was also found in the xenophobic anti-Semitism of the right-wing *Action française* movement of the turn of this century, which was not averse to characterizing Proudhon as one of the "Masters of the Nineteenth-century Counter Revolution" (cf. Introduction, p. 13 above).

rated earlier. I also substituted the principle of *balance* for that of *synthesis*. Until then I had shared Hegel's belief that the two terms of the antinomy, thesis and antithesis, were to become resolved in a superior term, *synthesis*. But I have since come to realize that just as the two poles of an electric cell do not destroy each other, so the two terms of the antinomy do not become resolved. Not only are they indestructible, but they are the very motive force of all action, life and progress. The problem is not to bring about their fusion, for this would be death, but to establish an equilibrium between them—an unstable equilibrium, that changes as society develops. I confessed this error quite plainly in my book *Justice,* as follows: "If my *System of Economic Contradictions* is not, as regards its method, a completely satisfactory work, it is because I had adopted Hegel's view of the antinomy. I thought that its two terms had to be resolved in a superior term, synthesis, distinct from the first two, thesis and antithesis. This was faulty logic as well as a failure to learn from experience, and I have since abandoned it. FOR THERE IS NO RESOLUTION OF THE ANTINOMY. This is the fundamental flaw in the whole of Hegel's philosophy. The terms are in a state of BALANCE, either with each other or with other antinomic terms, and this is what produces the desired result. But balance is not synthesis as Hegel understood it and as I too had supposed. Apart from this reservation made in the name of pure logic, I uphold today the rest of what I said in my *Contradictions*."

(1863–64)   *Property* pp. 49, 51–53

When you say that justice is not antinomic *in substance,* I agree with you, since its non-antinomic nature was what I was dealing with.

When you add that *in practice* it may be antinomic, you are saying in a different way what I said in my eighth and ninth studies [of *Justice*] when I said that consciousness, which is constant and invariable in substance, was sometimes forced to make judgments according to a *hypothetical law*. From this I deduced the theory of *progress*, that is to say, the movement of justice.

When you claim *to be going further than I have gone* in saying that *understanding is in substance no more antinomic than consciousness*, I think you are simply reproducing the basic idea of my new preface to the Brussels edition, in which I show that Justice is to consciousness as the principle of *equality* or *equation* is to the understanding. This principle is true of all intellectual operations. The antinomy is one of the phenomena or forms of the understanding. Equation is another form. These two forms activate each other, and it is because the first exists that the second also exists. But given that the body of knowledge implies equilibrium, that certitude is not equilibrium, that the intellectual movement resulting from the antinomy aims at an equilibrium, that reason reposes in equilibrium or knowledge, and that this equilibrium is in no way antinomic—for otherwise there would be no certainty, no truth, and thought would simply be a perpetual seesaw—the net result is that the understanding, like consciousness, which it includes, although it embraces all the antinomies cannot and must not be antinomic.

(January 17, 1862)   *C* 11, pp. 349–50

To Langlois

The causes of the uneasiness that is felt in society today are not merely accidental and peculiar to our age and nation. They are as old as the human race. They are a part of our constitution and can only be distinguished today from what they were yesterday by the more acute awareness of them experienced by a more advanced generation of men, and by the intensity of the ideas and antagonisms they produce.

I analyzed and developed most of these causes ten years ago in my principal work, called ECONOMIC *Contradictions*. To this I ought to add *Philosophical, Political, Religious* and *Legal Contradictions*.

The word *contradiction* is not meant in the ordinary sense, referring to a man who says something and then takes it back. It means, on the contrary, an opposition that is inherent in all the elements and forces of which society is composed. This opposition causes these forces to fight and destroy each other if man, through the exercise of reason, is unable to discover some way of understanding, controlling and maintaining them in a state of equilibrium.

(August 24, 1856)   *C* 7, pp. 116–17

To Emile Charpentier

Only when man has become reconciled with himself and ceases to regard his neighbor and nature as hostile forces will he be able to love and to create through the force of his spontaneity alone. Then he will desire to give, whereas today he desires only to acquire, and it will be in labor and devotion that he will seek his whole happiness and supreme pleasure. When that happens, when love becomes the true and only law governing mankind, justice will become a meaningless word, an unwelcome memory of an era of violence and tears.

I am not, of course, overlooking antagonism—or as you may like to call it, religious alienation—any more than the necessity of reconciling man with himself. In fact, my whole philosophy is one of perpetual reconciliation. You recognize the divergences within our nature as being the basic factor of society, or rather, the very stuff of civilization. It is the meaning of this indestructible fact, please note, that I seek. We would certainly be much nearer to reaching an understanding if instead of considering the dissonance and harmony of human faculties as occurring at two different times, separate and distinct in history, you would consent to share my view that these are simply the two sides of our nature, always opposed to each other, always working toward reconciliation, but never becoming completely reconciled. In short, just as individualism is the primordial factor in humanity, so association is its complementary term. Both are present constantly, and on earth there can be no love without justice.

Thus the doctrine of the Fall is not merely an expression of a particular, passing phase in human reason and morality. It is the spontaneous confession, in symbolic terms, of a fact that is as indestructible as it is amazing, namely, that the human race is guilty and inclines toward evil. The conscience of mankind cries out from every land and in every language: Woe be to me, O sinner. *Voe nobis quia peccavimus!* By giving this idea concrete and dramatic expression, religion has been able to transport what dwells within our inmost soul beyond the world and outside history. This is not just an intellectual delusion on the part of religion; religion is not mistaken about the essential and abiding truth of that fact.

(1846)   *Econ. Contrads.* I, pp. 368–69

If from marriage I move on to the family, and from the family to the State and go further and further into this organo-psychic mystery of a dual, plural personality, reason and experience lead me to conclude that society, like the individual and the couple, has a force, will and consciousness of its own. Thus I am led to consider society as being as real a thing as the individuals who compose it, and then to see the collectivity or group as the condition for all existence, and the series as the basis for all ideas and all concepts. Thus I acquire knowledge of material things through spiritual things. Similarly matter, simple and complex bodies and their forces, are merely, as the word *matter* indicates, the material embodiment of the moral order, the instrument and organic expression of Justice.

Finally, and this is rather surprising given the prejudices of my philosophical school, I reach an understanding of my FREE WILL and of all my most difficult ideas, with the help of the notions of the collective force, the group and the series. Thanks to the notion of free will which has at last been explained, I understand the *ideal* that delights me, and *progress* that is my guiding law.

This does not mean that man's evolution is determined by fate, but rather, that he will be freed indefinitely from all fatality. Through free will I can account for the origins of evil and the reasons why Justice diminishes and the nations decay. I can posit the principles of an aesthetic and of a philosophy of history.

I also become aware of the idea of *universal harmony*. I can see that everything in the world of Justice, law, force, and substance corresponds to the world of nature. The perfect order that reigns among the spheres in space, and the immutable distribution of the elements that make up all created things should be echoed in human affairs. The facts immediately confirm my hypothesis. Economics, politics, industrial organization, the public reason itself, all are integrated to form a system of checks and balances. In the analogy between the organization of the Cosmos and the Anthropos it becomes apparent that an identical spirit animates both. In the first case it is latent, in the second it has been liberated . . . .

We have to discover whether our idea of things corresponds to reality and whether the account our reason gives fits the reality of the phenomena.

In order to dispel any doubts about this, I would repeat what I have already observed. Namely, that what specifically constitutes the human self is Justice. Thus what we have to ask is whether the laws of understanding, which in man are external in origin and are consequently objective, that is to say they belong to the non-self, are the same in every respect as those of the consciousness, which alone constitutes our subjectivity; in other words, whether the notions that are the basis of all our knowledge are revelations of experience and embodiments of our moral sense, forms of thought and forms of Justice.

When phrased in these terms (and it would not be intelligible in any others) the problem becomes soluble. We only have to draw a simple conclusion.

Thus the *antinomy* which has been so widely used in the dialectic, and about which many illusions still persist, is a feature of our consciousness of law as well as of our understanding. We experience it first of all in our hearts in the love we feel for a woman, and then in our desire to emulate, which causes us to want to be treated in all things like other men, to weigh equally in *the balance* with them. This in Revolutionary terms is *being equal before the law*.

The *series* is a feature of our consciousness of law as well as being a law of our understanding. We experience this, too, deep in our hearts, firstly in our consciousness of the collectivity, that is, in family ties, and later in the collective force by virtue of which all of us, as workers, claim our share of the collective product, and, as citizens, our part in government, protesting against any exploitation of the individual and against all authority.

The principle of *causality* is a feature of our consciousness of law as well as of our understanding. We experience it in remorse, and so on.

Now the series, the antinomy, the notion of causality, the formulation of logic, all these are the component parts of logic and metaphysics. In this connection I must demonstrate that ethical axioms, which are present in the consciousness as well as in the understanding, are more elementary in nature than mathematical axioms. So economics, which derives directly from the latter, is a parallel feature of understanding, along with geometry, arithmetic and algebra, and it develops in the same way. I will not follow up these curious digressions.

Thus any metaphysical or speculative skepticism can only be countered by putting an end to skepticism about Justice. The self has to be centered not in the pure understanding, but in the consciousness. Next, the analysis of features peculiar to each faculty has to prove that the following fundamental propositions are one and the same thing: *the universe is founded on the laws of Justice*, and *Justice is organized in accordance with the laws of the universe.* Then these two propositions have to be formulated as one, namely, that THE SYSTEM OF THE LAWS OF JUSTICE IS THE SAME AS THE SYSTEM OF THE LAWS OF THE WORLD AND THEY ARE PRESENT IN THE HUMAN SOUL NOT ONLY AS IDEAS OR CONCEPTS BUT AS EMOTIONS OR FEELINGS.

(1858)   *Justice* IV, pp. 431–33

XVIII ON HISTORY AND THE IDEA OF PROGRESS

History

History, like philosophy, is not a science. It is not specialized, has no one object, method or series of its own. History is the succession of different states through which human intelligence and society pass before the former reaches pure science and the latter the application of science's laws. It is a panorama of creative activity in the making, a jumbled pattern of events which fuse and influence each other. It presents a series of more or less regular tableaux, until at last, when each idea has fitted into place and each constituent element of society has been elaborated and classified, the drama of revolution will draw to a close and history will become simply the record of scientific facts, of art forms and of industrial progress. Then the activities of the generations of men will be like the meditations of a recluse. Civilization will have donned the mantle of eternity.

(1843)   *Creation* pp. 357–58

Since[101] facts are needed to establish the certainty of the science of economics, our study of history must be based on labor . . . .

But when we have observed the influence of labor on society from the point of view of production and the movement of wealth, we must also trace its organic manifestations in revolutionary movements and various forms of government. We must find out whether, seen from this new angle, the facts deny or confirm the conclusions reached theoretically; whether the social system and all that this embraces, religious practices, war, commerce, science, art, etc., are in fact determined and constituted by the system of laws or organization as we have described it, or whether they are contradictory to it. In the light of this study we will draw up a topography of the various phases of humanity and see how far civilization has progressed to the present day by virtue of its own energy and its *providential* laws. Society is perpetually creating order. From the very first it traced a furrow which we cannot leave with impunity. Thus we must calculate its direction and its end if we are to continue

[101] At last the author is becoming intelligible. History is for him the same thing as Political Economy, considered from a particular angle. Therefore history is a science. (Proudhon's footnote)

successfully in the work which we began under God's very guidance.

(1843)   *Creation* pp. 369–70

There are two methods of studying history. One is what I will call the *providential* method, the other the *philosophical* method.

The first consists of attributing the cause of events either to a superior will that directs the course of things from on high, that is to God, or to a human will which is momentarily placed in such a position that, like God, it can affect the course of events through the exercise of its free will. This method does not totally exclude all design or systematic premeditation in history, but there is no necessity in the design and it could at any moment be revoked at its author's pleasure. It depends entirely upon the decisions of persons and on the sovereign will of God . . . .

It is clear that basically this is the same thing as the theory of chance. The believer may call it PROVIDENCE and the skeptic FORTUNE, but it is one and the same thing . . . .

While the philosophical method recognizes that there is no inevitability in particular events and that these may vary infinitely according to the individual wills that cause them to happen, it nevertheless holds that all events depend on general laws inherent in nature and in man. These laws constitute the eternal, unchanging meaning of history, while the particular facts that express these laws, like written characters that express the spoken word, or like words that express ideas, constitute the 'arbitrary face of history. They could be altered an infinite number of times without the immanent meaning they clothe being at all affected.

Thus my reply to the objection that has been raised is that the Provisional Government could have been composed of different men. Louis Blanc need not have been a member of it. Barbès and Blanqui[102] need not have added the complications of their rival influence to an already complex situation. The majority in the National Assembly could have been more democratic. These things and many others, I maintain, were possible, and things could have turned out very differently. This is what I mean by the accidental, *factitious* side of history.

But given the revolutionary series in which the modern world is engaged, a series that is itself the results of conditions imposed by human intelligence, and given a prejudice everyone both rejects and accepts, namely, that it is for the national authority to instigate and direct reform, I maintain that the events that must follow from this, whether fortunate or unfortunate, can only be the expression of the struggle that will inevitably take place between tradition and the Revolution . . . .

According to this philosophical conception of history, the main facts are arranged in a causal sequence and follow on from each other with a deductive rigor unsurpassed in the exact sciences. And since it is possible for reason to discover the philosophy behind the sequence, it is possible for human wisdom to direct its course. According to the providential theory on the other hand, history is merely a novelettish imbroglio devoid of all principle, reason and aim. It is an argument in favor of superstition

[102] Barbès and Blanqui were two leading revolutionary activists. They had led a demonstration on May 15, 1848, that had invaded the Constituent Assembly and included among its demands the abolition of property. Later, from the *Hôtel de Ville,* a new Government was proclaimed which included Proudhon's name as a member. Proudhon escaped arrest along with the demonstrators only because he had denounced their action in advance. When he was eventually imprisoned in June 1849, he came into contact with the revolutionaries and was able to observe Barbès and Blanqui, who he decided were more led by than leaders of the masses.

as well as atheism, an offense to the intelligence and consciousness.

(1849)   *Confessions* pp. 147–49

Progress

Order is maintained among creatures who do not organize themselves or who are devoid of intelligence by unconscious, blind, infallible forces and in accordance with laws of which they are ignorant. In intelligent beings it is through forces that are felt and which, for this very reason, are liable to vary in accordance with laws that these beings must necessarily discover.

In other words, brute beasts obey the laws that govern them without knowing it, while man's life is ordered only as the result of knowledge and deliberation, and, if I may put it in this way, only because he elaborates his own laws.

Now we do not acquire understanding of our laws in a moment and instinctively, but through sustained reflection, research and method.

As a result there have been three great stages in the development of human knowledge: the Religious, the Philosophical and the Scientific . . . .

By PROGRESS I mean the mind's upward movement, through the three successives stages of Religion, Philosophy and Metaphysics or method, toward Science.

(1843)   *Creation* pp. 36–37, 39

The closer man is to the beasts, the more deeply he is sunk into that miserable condition the philosophers of the last century termed a state of nature, the more he is forced to rely on the use of his own limbs and, as a result, the less he fulfills his potential and the less he works. Social progress is assessed in terms of the development of industry and the sophistication of tools. A man who cannot or does not know how to work with tools is an anomaly or a freak. He cannot be called a man.

(1843) *Creation* pp. 297–98

Really the logic of the socialists is quite amazing.

Man is good, they say, but in order to make him abstain from evil he must see no advantage in it. Man is good, but he must see some advantage in goodness if he is to practice it. For if the interest of his passions inclines him toward evil he will do evil, and if this same interest leaves him indifferent to the good, he will fail to do good. Society has no right to reproach him for having listened to his passions, for society should have guided him by means of his passions. What a richly endowed and refined nature Nero had. He killed his mother because the woman annoyed him, and had Rome burned so that he could have his own performance of the sack of Troy! What an artistic soul had Heliogabalus, who organized prostitution! What a forceful character Tiberias was! But what a terrible society it was that perverted these divine souls, and nevertheless produced Tacitus and Marcus Aurelius! . . . .

The moral perfecting of man, like his material well-being, takes place through a succession of oscillations between vice and virtue, *merit* and *demerit*.

Yes, man makes progress toward justice and thus toward liberty, but this progress is due entirely to the development of our intelligence and proves nothing about the goodness of our nature. Far from allowing us to worship our passions, it genuinely destroys their supremacy. Our maliciousness changes its form with the times. The feudal lords of the Middle Ages robbed the traveler on the highway and then offered him hospitality in their castles. The feudal lords of commerce are less brutal. They exploit the proletarian and then build hospitals for

him. Who would venture to say which of these deserves
the palm of virtue?

(1846)   *Econ. Contrads.* I, pp. 360, 362

I founded my judgments on the basic rule that if any
principle, when taken to its logical conclusion, ended in a
contradiction, then it should be considered as false and
rejected. Furthermore, if any institution had been founded
on such a principle, it should be considered as unsound or
utopian.

Armed with this criterion, I chose as my subject of experiment the oldest, most respectable, most universal and
least questioned institution in society, namely Property.
Everyone knows what happened. After a long, detailed
and above all impartial analysis, in the same way as a
mathematician working out his equations, I reached the
astonishing conclusion that property is, from whatever
angle you look at it, and whatever principle you refer it
to—a contradictory notion! Since denying property means
denying authority, I immediately deduced from my definition the no less paradoxical corollary that the true form of
government is *anarchy*. Finally, I discovered by a mathematical proof that no improvement can be made in social
economy through the force of society's primitive constitution alone, but that it must be aided and consciously desired by all. Thus I recognized that there comes a moment
in the life of all societies when progress, at first an unconscious process, requires the intervention of man's freely
exercised reason, and I concluded from this that the
spontaneous impetus we call Providence does not provide
the answer to everything. From that moment, although
I did not become what is rather unphilosophically termed
an atheist, I ceased to worship God . . . .

However, criticism must not only demolish, it must
also make positive assertions and reconstruct. If not, socialism would simply remain a subject of curiosity,

alarming to the bourgeoisie and of no use to the people . . . .

The method I had used for constructing [*sic:* presumably Proudhon meant to write "destroying"] was useless when it came to building. The process by which the mind affirms is not the same as that by which it denies. Before I could build anything I had to find a way out of the contradiction and create a revolutionary method of inventing, that is to say a philosophy that was not negative, but, to use Auguste Comte's expression, *positive*. It is only society, the collective body, that can follow its instinct and allow itself to exercise its own free will without fear of falling into complete and immediate error. Its own higher reason, which little by little becomes apparent in the actions of the masses and the thinking of individuals, always sees that it is set back on the right course. The philosopher, on the other hand, cannot discover the truth through intuition, and if what he is proposing to direct is society itself, he runs the risk of substituting his own inevitably faulty views for the eternal laws of order, and of toppling society into an abyss.

He needs a guide, and what could be a better one than the law of development, the very logic of humanity? Holding the thread of ideas in one hand and the thread of history in the other, I imagined that I would be able to penetrate the innermost meaning of society. I would become a prophet without ceasing to be a philosopher.

(1849)   *Confessions* pp. 173–74, 176–77

In human society instinct and reason, which are present there in parallel to each other, are both raised to their highest level. Humanity and Divinity are, in the Social Body, combined, but first of all they are antagonistic. The manifestations of instinct constitute Divine or Providential rule, while the manifestations of philosophy constitute the rule of liberty. Religions, empires, the poetry and monuments of the past are created by social spontaneity, which reason ceaselessly revises and rejuvenates.

But in society as well as in the individual, reason and reflection always triumph over instinct and spontaneity. This is the characteristic feature of our species and it accounts for the fact that we progress. It follows that Nature in us seems to retreat while Reason comes to the fore, or, in other words, God retires and Mankind advances.

(1849)   *Confessions* p. 182–83

The same thing can be said about love as about labor, property, exchange and everything in society. It is when man emerges from the state of nature that the concept of Justice is born and the city formed. This simply proves that the state of nature is for man an unnatural state, and all Jean-Jacques' pronouncements on the subject are absurd. Similarly, it is when man emerges from the state of nature and begins to live in society that property becomes distinct from theft, that exchange is legalized and frees itself from speculation and that labor is organized around the division and the group.

(1858)   *Justice* IV, p. 16

Do not expect me to provide you with a system. My system is Progress, that is to say the need to work constantly toward discovering the unknown while the past is being exhausted ... Next year this facet of our work, which is more important than any other, will be revealed in such a way as to strike people's minds. They will then understand that for us *free credit* and other formulae are merely the first steps away from the past, that the future, in all its fullness, remains obscure, and that we may scarcely do more than imagine it in the form of a more or less mythical symbol, which we call Anarchy and others

Fraternity. Then it will also become clear why sects and systems are of no significance, why the true revolutionary works only from day to day, and why man's destiny is an empty space, a hiatus in his path. Only children are amused by systematized perspectives. The Common People are just like this; they are unable to understand that man, like the Wandering Jew, must always be moving on. They seek repose with Cabet, Fourier, etc., beneath the shade of Communities and Associations. The Common People, like the reactionaries, want finality. But, I repeat, there is no finality, and if history is able to teach us anything about the curve we are at present describing, we nevertheless remain almost totally ignorant about the future. We cannot see beyond the antithesis that is suggested to us by the present.

This theory of Progress has been developed at length and excludes all absolute notions and all so-called definitive hypotheses; it must, in my opinion, form the solid but nevertheless fluid basis of the future. It will protect society from both the laziness of conservatism and from false revolutionary enterprises.

(December 1851)   C 4, pp. 157–58

To Langlois

If you wish, let us respect God's mystery; let us incline our will before his unquestionable decrees. But since he has allowed the world and ourselves to become the subject of our active spirit of inquiry, he doubtless also allows us to argue about the origin and cause of our disputes, even if the controversy will one day allow us to become as all-knowing as he. Let us therefore argue, and would to heaven that we had never done anything else . . . .

Let us consider together the two dimensions of history [the past and the future]. Together they form the Social System, which is complete, unbroken, and always consistent in all its parts. Its anomalies and accidents will serve to bring out the meaning of history, namely order.

Thus the social system considered as it really is and in its entirety, does not exist on a particular day and in a particular part of the world. It can only be revealed to us at the end of time. It will only be known to the last man on earth. We who belong to intermediate generations can only base our picture of it on conjectures of an increasingly accurate kind. The only thing that has been handed down to us, in the philosophy of man's progress, is that through a healthy understanding of our past we must ceaselessly prepare our future. Our fathers have given us a certain form of society. We will leave a different form to our grandchildren. This is the limit of our science, if such it be. These are the bounds within which we may exercise our liberty. Therefore it is upon ourselves that we must work if we wish to influence the destiny of the world. We must use the past as it has been left us by our ancestors while preserving the future of our descendants.

(1849)   Confessions pp. 69–71

We are not moving toward an ideal perfection or final state that we can attain in a single moment, when at death we cross its boundary. We are carried along with the universe in a constant process of development. The more we develop intellectually, the more certain and glorious this development will be. Progress is therefore the law of our souls, not only in the sense that through perfecting ourselves we constantly draw nearer to absolute Justice and the ideal, but also in the sense that since humanity, like creation itself, is ceaselessly changing and developing, the ideal of Justice and beauty we must attain is changing all the time.

Thus the contemplation of the infinite that seemed to be leading us toward quietism is precisely what prevented this from happening. We participate in universal, eternal life, and the more we reflect its image in our own lives through our actions and through Justice, the happier we shall be. The fact that our lives are so brief is not important. We live on through our descendants and they in turn are linked to the perpetual life of the universe. Even if this globe on which we live, which we are now almost certain had a beginning, were to shatter beneath our feet and be scattered in space, we ought not to consider this anything more than a local disturbance that would not in any way upset the system of the universe. It need not cause us any despair or at all affect our happiness. If the father on his deathbed is joyful in the knowledge that his children will live after him, why should not this be true of the human species, when it feels life drying up in the earth's soil and subsequently in its own veins? There will be other worlds after ours. Is this idea too difficult for the simple, or too simple for the philosophers?

(1858)   *Justice* I, p. 233

What dominates all my studies, constitutes their principle and their aim, their summit and their base—in short, their reason; what provides the key to all my controversies, to all my disquisitions and digressions and, finally, constitutes my originality as a thinker (if I may be permitted to claim that I have any) is that resolutely and irrevocably, in all things and everywhere, I proclaim *Progress,* and that no less resolutely, in all things and everywhere, I denounce the *Absolute*.

(1853)   *Progress* p. 45

Most learned men as well as ignorant people ordinarily understand Progress to mean something utilitarian and material. Roughly speaking, they take it to be the accumulation of discoveries, the multiplying of machines, the increase in general well-being, at the very best the spread of education and improvement of its methods. In short it represents increase in material and moral wealth and the possibility for an ever-increasing number of men to share the pleasures of riches and of the mind. Of course this too is Progress, and the philosophy of Progress would be most unfruitful and very shortsighted if it began its speculations by putting aside *the physical, moral and intellectual improvement of the poorest and most numerous class,* as Saint-Simon's phrase goes.[103] But all these things are only a very limited expression of Progress; an image, a symbol, or shall we say a product. Philosophically, such a notion of Progress is valueless.

Progress, I repeat, is an affirmation of universal movement, and thus it is the denial of all forms and formulae of immutability, all doctrines of eternity, irremovability and impeccability, etc., applied to any being whatsoever. It denies the permanence of any order, including that of the universe itself, and the changelessness of any subject or object, be it empirical or transcendental.

The Absolute or absolutism, on the contrary, affirms all that Progress denies, and denies all that Progress affirms. It is the search, in nature, society, religion, politics, morality, etc., for the eternal, the immutable, the perfect, the final, the unchangeable, the undivided. It is, to borrow a term that has become famous in our parliamentary debates, in all things and everywhere, the *status quo* . . . .

From these double and contradictory definitions of progress and the absolute, we may first deduce as a corollary a proposition that seems rather strange to our minds, which have been attuned for so long to absolutism. This is that the true, real, positive and practicable in all things is what changes, or at least what is capable of progression, reconciliation and transformation, while what is false, fictitious, impossible and abstract appears as fixed, com-

[103] Cf. note 61, p. 168.

plete, whole, unchangeable, indefectible, not capable of modification, conversion, increase or decrease, and is thus refractory to any greater combination or synthesis.

(1853)   *Progress* pp. 49–50

XIX   ON JUSTICE

In order to regulate relations between people, to allow them to live together in a state of interdependence and thus to create society, we need some principle, some power or entity, something like what we call Justice, having its own reality and its own institutions through which to determine people's wills and impose its laws . . . .

It has been claimed that Justice is simply a relation of balance, conceived by the understanding but freely accepted by the will, in the same way as any other intellectual speculation, on account of its usefulness. And thus it is claimed that Justice, when reduced to its basic formula, is simply a precautionary measure or safeguard, an act of good will or even of sympathy which is always motivated by self-interest. Apart from this it is pure imagination . . . .

Now we may conceive of the reality of Justice in two ways. Either it is an external, objective pressure exerted on the self, or it is a faculty of the self which, although subjective, would make a man as keenly aware of his neighbor's dignity as of his own. Thus, while retaining his own individuality, he would become identified with the collective being itself . . . .

The first and older of these two systems, still supported by most of the peoples of the world although it is daily losing ground among the civilized nations, is the TRANSCENDENTAL system, commonly known as *Revelation*. All religions and quasi-religions aim at inculcating this system . . . .

The other system, which is radically opposed to the first and which was the aim of the Revolution, is that of IMMANENCE, which believes Justice innate to human consciousness.

According to this theory, man, although he was originally in a completely savage state, constantly creates society through the spontaneous development of his nature. It is only in the abstract that he may be regarded as in a state of isolation, governed by no law other than self-interest. His consciousness is not, as the transcendentalists[104] teach, of a dual nature, part animal and part divine. It is simply polarized. Man is an integral part of collective existence and as such he is aware both of his own dignity and that of others. Thus he carries within himself the principles of a moral code that goes beyond the individual. He does not receive these principles from elsewhere. They are intimately and *immanently* part of himself. They constitute his essence and the essence of society itself. They are the characteristic mold of the human soul, daily refined and perfected through social relations.

In a word, Justice is a part of ourselves just as love, the notions of the beautiful, the useful and the true, and all our capabilities and faculties are parts of ourselves. Since nobody dreams of attributing love, ambition, speculation or business sense to God, why should we make an exception of Justice?

Justice is human, totally human and nothing but human and we wrong it if we attribute it, directly or indirectly, to a principle that is above man and exists prior to him. Let philosophers busy themselves as much as they like with the nature of God and his attributes. This is probably their right and their duty. I maintain that the notion

[104] Cf. note 39, p. 122.

of God has no place in our legal constitutions any more than in our treatises on political economy or algebra. The theory of *Practical Reason* exists of itself. It neither presupposes nor requires the existence of God or the immortality of the soul. It would be false if it needed props of this kind.

(1858) *Justice* I pp. 315–16, 323–24

Need I add that according to this theory, since man must acquire his knowledge of Justice by himself, entirely by himself, his knowledge is necessarily progressive, being revealed to him little by little through experience? This is unlike revealed knowledge which is given once and for all so that not one iota can be added to it or subtracted from it. The history of lawmaking, moreover, proves this theory of the progressive knowledge of Justice . . . .

Now, since progress is postulated firstly as a condition of knowledge and next as synonymous with the increase of Justice, everything in human history—its fluctuations and deviations, its stumblings and its recoveries—can be explained, down to the negation of human potential that all religions are based on, and down to the ensuing despair of Justice that, while purporting to call us to God, in fact finally destroys all morality.

Thus from *practical philosophy*, or the search for laws governing human action, we may deduce the *philosophy of history*, or the search for the laws of history. This latter could equally well be termed *historiology*, which is to *historiography*—the description of historical facts—as anthropology is to ethnography.

(1858) *Justice* I p. 327

There is one point on which I find both what you have written down and the thought behind it, inaccurate. It is where you talk about the *antinomy of Justice*. It is quite certain that, like political economy, metaphysics, etc., the science of laws turns on constant antinomies. In this sense your expression is justified and your article[105] very clearly explains what this antinomy is in people's rights and in war. But in fact this antinomy does not derive from Justice itself. Consciousness, like understanding, is not antinomic by nature. If this were the case, there would be no such thing as positive morality and we would have to accept the laissez-faire of the Malthusians. Justice, in itself, is the balance of antinomies; that is to say, it holds the conflicting forces in a state of equilibrium and *equates* their respective claims. This is the reason why I have not made *liberty* my motto, for liberty is an indefinite, absorbing force that may be crushed though not defeated. Above it I placed Justice which judges, regulates and distributes. Liberty is the collective, sovereign force, and Justice is its law.

(December 30, 1861)   *C* 11, p. 308

To Langlois

Until now, in fact, theologians and philosophers have agreed to deduce the principles of law and morals from some theological or metaphysical hypothesis, theory or doctrine, call it what you will. For all of them, morals are founded on dogma. Practical reason is derived from speculative reason, which provides practical reason, through its rules, with its certainties. The reason for this is that Justice has never been thought of as anything but a category of reason, like time, space, causality, substance, the beautiful, the useful, and so on. At most they called it one of God's commandments, and this was quite in keeping with their thesis.

I, on the contrary (and I think that this is why my

---

[105] Which was a critique by Langlois of Proudhon's book on *Justice*.

work is original), hold that morality exists by itself and is not derived from any dogma or theory. Consciousness[106] is man's principal faculty, his sovereign power, served by all the other faculties. Similarly, I hold that it is not religion that makes man, nor the political system that makes the patriot or the citizen. It is quite the reverse. Man makes religions and the citizen makes the State. And again, I do not draw the rules of my life or my social existence from any metaphysic, aesthetic or theodicy. On the contrary, I derive the laws of my understanding from the dictates of my conscience;[106] in my conscience I find sanctions for my opinions and proof of my certainty. The notion of what is just is, as I see it, both an idea and a feeling. Since feeling is the first expression and principal force in my life, outside which I find only shame and misery, it seemed logical to me to overturn the teaching I had received from childhood. Instead of making my duty and law depend on the more or less precarious state of my reason, I decided to subject my reason and opinion to my feeling of duty and law.

My mind naturally tends to work this way and it has done so since I was a child. Long before I was aware of it, this approach informed and directed my criticism. It explains all my negations and affirmations. I soon discovered that the advantage of this method over normal methods was that I could be mistaken in my ideas without feeling shame or great regret, while I could not make mistakes about things relating to conscience without feeling some guilt and torment. Furthermore I can bear to see my ideas universally rejected and mercilessly criticized without feeling that it is the end of the world. Whereas if Justice, which I worship, is spurned and violated, I am consoled by the torture to which the defaulters are in-

---

[106] *La conscience*, i.e. "consciousness" or "conscience," and Proudhon uses it in both senses in this passage.

stantly put, even if they are very powerful and very wealthy, and even if they constitute the greater part or even the whole of the nation. The result is that my own religion or my philosophy, if I may put it in these ambitious terms, will never be irrevocably condemned. Society cannot desire its own death. Thus I feel that I am in communion with the whole human race and that all past centuries are in communion with me.

(1858)   *Justice* IV pp. 492–93

XX   THE PEASANT FAMILY

Marriage

When I was forty I married a working girl who was young and poor. Since you are well acquainted with the nature of my feelings, you can well imagine that I did not do it through passion. It was through sympathy for her situation and esteem for her person. It was because my mother had died and I was without a family—and because, although you may not believe it, even if I was not in love, I cherished the idea of a *household* and PATERNITY. I did not think further than this.

Over four years my wife's gratitude has given me three little fair-haired, rosy-cheeked daughters. Their mother nursed them herself and today they are the source of almost all my joy. I do not mind how often people tell me that I have been imprudent, that it is not enough to bring children into the world, one must bring them up and provide for their future. I only know that fatherhood has filled an enormous emptiness in my life, that it has given me a ballast I lacked, and energy such as I never knew.

1*

I regret that in '48 I had not already been a father for at least five or six years.

(March 5, 1854)   C 6, p. 3

To Bergmann

Marriage is the union of the two heterogeneous elements, *power* and *grace*. Man the producer, inventor, scholar, warrior, administrator or magistrate is the embodiment of the former. The latter is embodied in woman, of whom all one can say is that by nature she is destined to be the living idealization of all the qualities that man possesses in a higher degree, in the three spheres of labor, knowledge and rights. This is why women want men to be strong, brave and clever. They ignore them if they are merely kind and sweet. And this is why men want women to be beautiful, gracious, modest in speech, discreet and chaste . . . .

It thus follows that the union between man and woman is not a synallagmatic agreement in the manner of the usual contract of mutuality. Such a contract presupposes that the contracting parties or those engaged in the exchange are fully independent individuals of like kind and of equal status in the eyes of the law, in whose name they are coming together or negotiating the exchange of their services and products. Man and woman together, in both the moral and physical sense, form one organic whole composed of two persons, one soul endowed with two minds and two wills. The aim of this organism is to create Justice by stimulating consciousness, and to enable mankind to perfect itself by itself, that is to say civilization and all its wonders. How will this progress toward Justice be brought about? It will be by encouraging the ideal that theologians call grace and poets love. This is the theory. The time when people's feeling for Justice is most keen is the time they are of an age to love. Of course woman's beauty fades with the years, and man becomes subject to other influences. But once he has known Justice, he never forsakes it. It is a fact that corruption in society never springs from the generations who have known what it is to love but springs from those who have not yet known love or from those in whom love has been transformed into sensual pleasure. If modesty and love were to be taken away from youth, and lust put in their place, young people would very soon lose all sense of morality. They would become a race given over to servitude and infamy . . . .

Are men and women made equal as a result of their union? *Yes*, from the point of view of dignity and happiness, in the intimacy of the bridal chamber and in their hearts, they are equal. Marriage, which is founded on mutual and absolute devotion, entails the sharing of fortune and honor. But this equality does not and cannot exist in *social and public life*, in anything to do with the business and organization of life, or with the administration and defense of the republic. To put it more clearly, woman does not count in these spheres. She is considered as part of her husband. Why should this be so? One reason is that her faculties do not bear any comparison with those of a man in the realms of economics and industry, philosophy and literature, or in that of law. These three realms, which are the categories of the useful, the true and the just, account for three quarters of man's social activity. Thus society does no injustice to woman by refusing her equality before the law. It treats her according to her aptitudes and privileges. Woman really has no place in the world of politics and economics. Her function begins beyond these spheres. You will rejoin that she regains the advantage through her grace and beauty and the influence these enable her to exercise. True, and I repeat that it is not up to society, which is concerned with military matters, government, philosophy and law, to make any compensations. The State or society, call it what you will, does not and cannot recognize those things pertaining to the ideal and to love. The husband, as society's representative to woman, must compensate his wife. This he does, but not on the open market, and he uses different coin—the complete sacrifice of himself, in other words, his conjugal love. If you alter this system you alter the natural order of things. You impoverish man without giving woman more dignity or more happiness. Equality of civil and political rights would mean that the privileges and grace that nature has bestowed on woman would become bound up with man's utilitarian faculties. The result of this bargaining would be that woman, instead of being elevated, would become denatured and debased. By the ideal nature of her being, woman is, so to speak, of priceless value. She can reach greater heights than man, but only on condition that he raises her up. If she is to retain her inestimable grace, which is not a productive faculty or a value that can be exchanged but a transcendent quality, she must respect the force of the laws of marriage. If she were to be on an equal footing with man in public life, he would find her odious and ugly. This would mean the end of the institution of marriage, the death of love and the ruin of the human race.

(1858)   *Justice* IV, pp. 276–79

Thus man reproduces his body and soul, thoughts, feelings and actions by dividing his being. Since woman is one with him in consciousness, she is one with him in giving birth. The family, the extension of the conjugal couple, helps to develop the area in which Justice operates. The State, coming into existence through intermarriage between families, extends this with greater force. Marriage, the family and the State are all one and the same entity. The destiny of society is bound up with the destiny of the institution of marriage, and each one of us, as members of this universal communion, shares in the life of the whole human race.

(1858)   *Justice* IV, p. 302

On Poverty

There is no doubt that production has increased considerably during the last forty years. Probably it is proportionally greater today than it was in 1820. Nevertheless, there is no doubt that for people who were alive under the Restoration, hardship is greater today in all classes of society than it was in the reign of Louis XVIII. What is the reason for this? It is because the mode of living in the middle and lower classes has become more refined. At the same time, the laws of equilibrium are increasingly forgotten and violated, the laws of temperance are trampled under foot, so that poverty has become more burdensome; instead of being beneficial, as nature intended, it has become a form of torture. We have overdone our excesses and now we no longer have even the necessities of life . . . .

Thus it is the natural destiny of all nations, whether civilized or barbarian, and whatever their institutions and forms of government, to be poor. The further they move away from their primitive state—which is one of *abundance*—and progress by means of labor toward WEALTH, the poorer they become. As the population of the United States of America increases and takes possession of the land, the proportion of natural resources diminishes and the law of labor becomes more pressing. Furthermore, and this is a certain sign of poverty, things originally given away for nothing, or for next to nothing, are becoming more and more costly; primitive gratuity is disappearing, the system of VALUE is predominant, and already a proletariat is beginning to form . . . .

You ask whether industrial progress, always subject to

the laws of necessity, does not, since it provides subsistence for an increasing population, mean an improvement in the lot of the individual. Of course the lives of individuals are improved. But what form does this improvement take? For the spirit, it is an increase in knowledge, justice and the ideal; for the flesh, it is in more selective consumption, in keeping with the education of the mind.

Horses eat oats, cattle hay, pigs acorns, and hens grain. Their foodstuff never changes, but they do not find this disturbing. I have seen the laborer in the fields take his daily meal of the same black bread, the same potatoes, the same dish of meal, without appearing to suffer from it. It is only overwork that makes him thin. The civilized worker, on the other hand, who has received the first enlightening rays of the Word, needs some variety in his diet. He eats wheat, rice, maize, vegetables, meat, fish, eggs, fruit and dairy produce. He now and then drinks wine, beer, cider, mead, tea and coffee. He adds salt and seasoning to his food and prepares it in many different ways. Instead of simply covering himself with the sun-dried skin of a sheep or a bear, he wears clothes woven from wool, hemp, or cotton. He uses linen and flannel and has different clothing for summer and winter. His body is no less vigorous, but it is of nobler blood and indicates the culture his mind has acquired, and it demands attentions that the savage goes without. This is progress. But it does not mean that poverty is no longer man's lot. He still has not all he needs, and he cannot lose a day's labor without immediately feeling hunger pangs . . . .

You are dazzled by the elegance of towns, the colossal fortunes, the splendor of the State, the budget for the army and public works, the endowments, the Civil List, the hubbub of the banks, the Stock Exchange with its millions and thousands of millions, and by the heady revels of which you sometimes hear stories. These things dazzle you, and because they make you believe in wealth they sadden you in your poverty. Reflect, then, that all this magnificence is taken off the miserable average daily wage of 3 francs 50 centimes earned by a family of four, and that it is deducted from the laborer's product before his wages are fixed. The army budget is raised by taxation on labor, the national revenue is raised by taxation on labor, the money from property is raised by taxation on labor. The budget of the banker, the contractor, the trader or the public servant is raised by taxation on labor. The money spent on luxury is likewise raised by taxation on necessities. So have no regrets. Manfully accept your situation and tell yourselves, once and for all, that the happiest of men are those who best know how to be poor.

The wisdom of the ancients had an inkling of these truths. Christianity was the first to set out formally the law of poverty by giving it a theological interpretation, as is to be expected of any mysticism. In its reaction against the sensuality of paganism, however, it failed to consider poverty from its true vantage point. Poverty became associated with suffering through the Christian abstinences and fasts, with squalor because of the monks, with the curses of heaven because of the practice of performing expiations. But apart from this, the glorification of poverty in the Gospel is the greatest truth that Christ ever preached to men.

Poverty is seemly. Its clothes are not in holes like the mantle of the cynic. Its dwelling is clean, healthy and in good repair. It changes its linen at least once a week, and it is neither pale nor starving . . . .

Poverty is not *ease*. For the worker this would be a form of corruption. It is not good for man to live in ease. He must, on the contrary, always feel the pricks of need. Ease would be worse than corruption, it would be servitude. It is also important that man should, on occasion, rise above need, and even do without necessities. For all that, poverty has its own joys, its innocent festivities and homely luxuries which are all the more touching as they emphasize the customary frugality of the household.

It is clear that it would be misplaced to dream of escaping from the inevitable poverty that is the law of our nature and of society. Poverty is good, and we must think of it as being the source of all our joys. Reason demands that we should live with it—frugally, modifying our pleasures, laboring assiduously and subordinating all our appetites to justice.

(1861)   *War* pp. 334–39

The Land

Land belongs to the race of people born on it, since no other is able to develop it according to its needs. The Caucasian has never been able to take root in Egypt. Our northern races are no more successful in Algeria. The Anglo-Saxon looks quite different in America, where he becomes a Redskin. As to the mixing of races, this, when it can take place, far from destroying the native race, gives it a new lease on life and more vitality and vigor. We know today that blood can be mixed but that it does not become *fused.* One of the two races always ends by reverting to type and absorbing the other.

From this relationship between race and soil, which is the basis of all collective territorial possession, it is easy to deduce the idea of *individual possession,* subject, however, to more complicated conditions than national possession.

Lastly, collective and individual possession leads to a third principle, which the lawmakers of old glimpsed rather than defined, which the Utopians sacrificed and which society today is in the process of losing despite desperate efforts to retain it: this is *the hereditary principle.*

Thus man and the land, like Adam and Eve in Genesis,

can say to each other: "bone of my bone and flesh of my flesh." Partners in marriage, united in destiny and customs, together they produce their offspring. And who can say whether the sons of woman or the fruits of the earth should more rightly be called children of the earth or children of men?

(1858)   *Justice* II, pp. 389–90

People are no longer attached to the land as they used to be because they inhabit it, because they cultivate it, because they breathe its air and live on its substance, because like their blood they inherit it from their fathers and because they will hand it down through their descendants; nor because they derive their body, their temperament, their instincts, their ideas, their characters from it and could only separate themselves from it on pain of death. People are attached to the land as they are attached to a tool, or even less than that, to something which enables them to levy a certain revenue each year. Gone is the deep feeling for nature, the love of the soil, that only country life can give. In its place is the conventional sensibility peculiar to blasé societies who know nature only as it appears in the novel, the salon or the theater . . . .

Men no longer love the soil. Landowners sell it, lease it, divide it into shares, prostitute it, bargain with it and treat it as an object of speculation. Farmers torture it, violate it, exhaust it and sacrifice it to their impatient desire for gain. They never become one with it.

We have lost our feeling for nature. Our generation loves the fields and the woods as the magpie loves the gold it steals. We want them only for their investment value, so that we can indulge our rustic fantasies and build country nursing homes, or so we can experience pride of possession and be able to say "this is mine." We no longer feel the powerful attraction and sense of communion that exists between man and nature. The sirocco of Christianity has passed over our souls and parched them . . . .

Nevertheless, man loves nature more deeply than anything else. I will not try to explain this love—indeed who can explain love—but it is a genuine love, and like all real sentiments it has its own mythology.

The cults of the Sky, the Stars, and the Earth, the great mother of all things—*magna parens rerum*—Cybele, Tellus, Vesta, Rhea and Ops, were all hymns of love to nature . . . .

Nor, believe me, does love die with mythology. Morality does not cease when the philosopher ceases his prayers. Beauty is not destroyed for the anatomist by the presence of a corpse . . . .

If man and nature do not share a common essence, if our soul, radically different from matter, is to be considered as a simple and consequently amorphous thing whose only attribute is movement in all directions, then it follows that man, reduced to a state of total liberty, must not allow himself to be constrained by any laws. It follows that—like God himself, who before he had created the matter of the universe through his omnipotence, had created its laws through his intelligence—morality is governed by whim. Consequently man's condition is that of a tyrant, or rather, since he cannot destroy God's works, that of a captive, fallen soul, and his only dignity comes from his religion. Moreover, since the domination of mind over inert, passive matter is absolute, there are no such things as authentic or necessary forms in either economics or politics. Arbitrariness is the natural state of society.

(1858)   *Justice* II, pp. 397–400

XXI PROUDHON THE IRONIST

What our generation lacks is not a Mirabeau, a Robespierre, or a Bonaparte, but a Voltaire. We are incapable of assessing anything detachedly or mockingly. We are enslaved by our opinions as well as by our interests. As a result of taking ourselves seriously we are growing stupid. Increasing freedom of thought is the most precious fruit of scientific knowledge, but we are turning this knowledge into pedantry; instead of liberating our minds it is deadening them. We are so completely engrossed in our loves and our hates that we no more laugh at others than at ourselves. By having lost our wits, we have lost our liberty.

Liberty produces everything in the world. I repeat, everything; even those things it is destroying today: religion, government, nobility, property.

Like its sister, Reason, which has no sooner constructed a system than it starts to broaden its scope and reconstruct it, Liberty continually tries to change its previous creations. It tries to free itself from the forms it has adopted and to discover new ones, and then to liberate itself from these exactly as before, regarding them with dislike as being pitiful until it has replaced them by something new.

Liberty, like Reason, can only exist and be apparent through constantly rejecting its own creations. It perishes as soon as it begins to admire itself. This is why irony has always been the mark of the philosophical and liberal spirit, the seal of human intelligence and the irresistible instrument of progress. Static peoples are all solemn peoples. The common man who laughs is a thousand times closer to reason and liberty than the anchorite who prays, or the philosopher who spends his time in argument.

Irony, you are true liberty! You preserve me from aspirations to gain power, from being a slave to parties, from pedantry in science, from the admiration of the great, from the mystifications of politics, from the fanaticism of reformers, from the superstitions of this vast universe and from self-adoration. In the past you appeared to the Sage on the throne when he cried out, before all the people who saw him as a demigod, "Vanity of vanities." You were the familiar spirit of the Philosopher when at one blow he unmasked the dogmatist, the sophist, the hypocrite, the atheist, the epicurean and the cynic. You were the consolation of the Righteous One when, as he was dying, he prayed on the Cross for his executioners, saying, "Father, forgive them, for they know not what they do."

Sweet irony! You alone are pure, chaste and sober.

You add grace to beauty and seasoning to love. You inspire charity through tolerance and rid one of murderous prejudice. You teach women modesty, warriors daring and statesmen prudence. With your smile you appease dissension and civil war. You make peace between brothers and cure the fanatic and the sectarian. You are mistress to Truth, the protector of Genius, and you are, O goddess, Virtue itself.

Come, O sovereign, shed a ray of your light over my fellow citizens. Kindle in their hearts a spark of your spirit so they may be reconciled through my confession and so that the revolution, which is inevitable, may take place in serenity and joy.

(1849)   *Confessions* pp. 341–42

BIBLIOGRAPHY

This list includes only books on or by Proudhon that are available in English. Woodcock, in his biography of Proudhon, gives a more extensive bibliography of works in both English and French. P. Ansart's *Sociologie de Proudhon*, Paris, 1967, can also be consulted for further reading.

ENGLISH TRANSLATIONS OF PROUDHON

The Works of P.-J. Proudhon in English, translated and published by Benjamin R. Tucker: Vol. 1, *What Is Property?*, Princeton, 1876; republished by Howard Fertig, New York, 1966; Vol. 4, *System of Economical Contradictions or the Philosophy of Misery,* Boston, 1888. This covers only the first of the two volumes of the French edition.

General Idea of the Revolution in the Nineteenth Century, tr. John Beverley Robinson, London and Berlin, 1923.

Proudhon's Solution of the Social Problem, ed. Henry Cohen, with Commentary and Exposition by Charles A. Dana and William B. Greene, New York, 1927. This is a selection of Proudhon's writings on mutual banking taken from his *Solution du problème social, Système des contradictions économiques,* and *Organisation du crédit.*

WORKS IN ENGLISH ON PROUDHON

The most complete account of Proudhon's life and thought is that by George Woodcock, *Pierre-Joseph Prou-*

dhon: A Biography (London: Routledge and Kegan Paul, 1956); the same author devotes a chapter to Proudhon in his *Anarchism* (London: Penguin Press, 1963). Excellent chapters on Proudhon can be found in James Joll, *The Anarchists* (London: Eyre and Spottiswoode, 1964 and Boston: Atlantic-Little, Brown, 1965); G. D. H. Cole, *A History of Socialist Thought,* Vol. 1, *The Forerunners: 1789–1850* (London: Macmillan, 1953); and J. S. Schapiro, *Liberalism and the Challenge of Fascism: Social Forces in England and France, 1815–1870* (New York: McGraw-Hill, 1949). The misleading English title of Henri de Lubac's *The Un-Marxian Socialist: A Study of Proudhon* (London: Sheed and Ward, 1948), a translation of *Proudhon et le Christianisme* (Paris: 1945), covers an extended and powerful interpretation of Proudhon's ethical philosophy. Studies of Proudhon's political ideas can be found in D. W. Brogan, *Proudhon* (London: H. Hamilton, 1934); S. Y. Lu, *The Political Theories of P. J. Proudhon* (New York: 1922); and Preston Theodore King, *Fear of Power: An Analysis of Anti-Statism in Three French Writers* (London: Cass, 1967), which relates Proudhon to de Tocqueville and Sorel. General surveys of European socialism are J. H. Jackson, *Marx, Proudhon and European Socialism* (London: Teach Yourself History Series, 1957) and David Caute, *The Left in Europe Since 1789* (London: Weidenfeld, 1966 and New York: McGraw-Hill, 1966). The first volume of G. D. H. Cole's *History of Socialist Thought,* cited above, has chapters on the ideas of the French socialists of Proudhon's time; the first chapter of Val R. Lorwin, *The French Labor Movement* (Cambridge: Harvard University Press, 1954), gives a brief account of the same period. The opening chapters of Gordon Wright, *Rural Revolution in France* (Stanford University Press, 1964), can be consulted on the French peasantry.

The political and social history of nineteenth-century France can be most conveniently approached through

A. B. C. Cobban, *A History of Modern France* (London: Penguin Books, 1965), Vol. 2. Although it goes only to 1848, several chapters in E. J. Hobsbawm, *The Age of Revolution: Europe 1789–1848* (London: Weidenfeld, 1962), give a valuable picture of economic developments and of the origins of the European labor and nationalist movements. Karl Marx's *The Poverty of Philosophy* (Moscow: Foreign Languages Publishing House, 1956) as well as Chapter 4 of *The Holy Family* (Moscow: Foreign Languages Publishing House, 1956) refer to Proudhon; the latter work antedates the correspondence between Marx and Proudhon given in the text. Proudhon's writings on the 1848 Revolution and the *coup d'état* of Napoleon III may be compared to Marx's interpretation of the same events in his *The Class Struggles in France*, and *The Eighteenth Brumaire of Louis Bonaparte;* and to de Tocqueville's *Recollections*, ed. J. P. Mayer (London: Mayflower, 1960; revised edition, New York: Doubleday, 1969).

INDEX